I FELL IN LOVE WITH YOUR MOM ON A BUS IN INDIA

Dear Kara,

Thank you for being such a nice friend to Jackie!

XO

I FELL IN LOVE WITH YOUR MOM ON A BUS IN INDIA

A Memoir of Love, Adventure, and Family

BARRY HOFFNER

Personal History
PRODUCTIONS LLC

ISBN-13: 978-0-9965590-6-5

Maps by Sarah Fiske

Produced by Personal History Productions LLC
707.539.5559
www.personalhistoryproductions.com

Personal History
PRODUCTIONS LLC

I dedicate this memoir, my manifesto of love, to my wife, Jackie Hoffner, the person to whom I owe everything.

It is written for you, my dear sons, Benjamin and Daniel, to underscore the profound love that I will always have for your blessed mother. As for my feelings for you both, you can never possibly understand the depth of love that Mom and I have for you.

Additionally, I also hope that my reflections of abiding love for my dear wife may in some small way encourage my friends, particularly male friends, to never leave anything unsaid. I regularly tell myself that I would give every single material thing I own just to have five minutes to tell Jackie how much she meant to me.

Contents

List of Maps

Preface

Aside from the pain of losing a beloved family member, it is hard to face the possibility of losing the memories with one's beloved spouse that only a husband or wife can truly relate to. Reading the stories written about my dear wife, Jackie Hoffner, by her parents, Diane and Lyell Holmes, I resolved to record for my boys, Benjamin and Daniel, the memories I shared with their mother. I certainly do not see myself as a writer, nor am I particularly fond of writing. However, for history's sake, I wanted my boys to know the joy, love, and adventure I shared with their dear mother from the time that Jackie and I met until the boys were of age to retain family memories. This memoir begins when I met Jackie at UC Irvine in 1981. It ends when we moved from Moscow, Russia, to Sausalito, California, in 2002. Benjamin and Daniel were three and four years old at that time.

This project started as a small personal one. I expected the writing to be no more than ten to fifteen pages that would record the experiences Jackie and I had mostly traveling and living in different places. That all changed when I unexpectedly found my dear wife's meticulously and vividly written diary, which she kept from the time we started traveling together toward the end of 1994 through mid-1996. During the period of time that she kept a regular diary—roughly twenty months—Jackie and I had a lifetime of memories, traveling to six countries in Asia (including living in China for four months), two countries in Australasia, nine countries in Africa, and five countries in Europe (including living in London for five months).

Without my dear wife's amazing descriptions of people, places, and relationships (including our own), this writing project would be of interest only to my boys and close family. However, Jackie's strong voice and exceptional character have motivated me to share this love story more broadly. Little is more important to me in my life than honoring my blessed wife and keeping her memory alive. I hope this memoir will do just that. During my own personal healing journey, partly through writing this memoir, I have gained a tremendous amount of strength and comfort from reliving the life we shared, both the early years of our relationship and our time together raising two wonderful boys.

I thank my close Cloverdale friends Roy and Janet for their encouragement, advice, and help in editing. I also thank Personal History Productions LLC, particularly Andi Reese Brady, for the enthusiastic, professional, and immeasurable help in finalizing and producing this memoir. Finally, I appreciate the input from my friends and family who contributed to this story.

Introduction for My Boys

Dear Benjamin and Daniel,

After Mom's tragic passing in Botswana on November 14, 2017, as I traveled from Dubai to Seville to pick you up, Daniel, and then, two days later to Washington, DC, for us to reunite with Benjamin as a family, I contemplated what I could possibly say to the two of you that would make any sense. I wanted the three of us to grieve together as a family. On top of the shock, devastation, and crushing heartbreak that gripped me, I was absolutely overwhelmed with how to comfort you both. I knew I had to pull myself together, say something that mattered, and initiate a discussion of our own personal and collective grief, but I had no idea how to approach this.

It was November 17, and I had hardly slept or eaten since I received that shattering phone call on the 14th in a hotel room in Dubai. Less than twelve hours later I was supposed to get on a flight from Dubai to meet Mom in Nairobi to visit together the Sheldrick Wildlife Trust, an elephant orphan rescue and rehabilitation center. My heart was absolutely broken for you both as well as for Mom's family. I carried that heartbreak with me when I had to inform countless people—including you two, the rest of our family, and Mom's many friends—of her tragic passing. I will always carry this heartbreak.

Finally, as the flight from Madrid to DC took off, with Daniel asleep next to me, a forceful wave of emotions hit me. I can only describe them as all the memories I had of your mother and us as a family, literally thousands of dreamlike recollections. Though I was in tears, sobbing, these memories kept playing over and over in my mind as if I were watching a movie, and they buoyed me with vivid remembrances of a blessed life. I felt the most powerful sense of gratitude. It was a sacred place of exceptionally profound consciousness that I could have never known existed until that moment. I knew that my deep love for your mother, that goes well-beyond her being with me physically, would somehow sustain me and give me the strength to get through this horrible tragedy. I asked myself then—and still do today—how it was possible that I could be feeling such spiritual strength after a devastating loss. It was at that moment that I finally knew what the concept of God meant to me personally. GOD = Love + Gratitude. We each hold that equation with us in our hearts but are seldom able to access it in our conscious thoughts in such a powerful way!

While I listened to some soothing music on the flight, the following words hit me: "Dear Benjamin and Daniel, even with my deep grief, I can't help but also feel so much gratitude for dear Mom's presence in our lives. I'll take those twenty-five years I got to spend with Mom over anything. And I want you both to know that my single greatest hope for you both, far ahead of all others, is that you will find love in a partner as I found in your blessed mother." If there is one thing that I have learned in my life, that I believe in more than anything, it is this: **love is transformational.** *I am living testimony to that! One of my personal heroes, Viktor Frankl, while in the Auschwitz concentration camp and separated from his wife, said it best.*

> For the first time in my life I saw the truth as it is set into song by so many poets, proclaimed as the final wisdom by so many thinkers. The truth—that love is the ultimate and highest goal to which man can aspire. Then I grasped the meaning of the greatest secret that human poetry and human thought and belief have to impart: The salvation of man is through love and in love. I understood how a man who has little left in this world may still know bliss, be it only for a brief moment, in contemplation of his beloved.

I still keep thinking about how the words to the song I listened to that day, "Perfect," by Ed Sheeran, describe exactly how I feel about Mom: "I have faith in what I see, now I know I have met an angel, in person, and she looks perfect."

I FELL IN LOVE WITH YOUR MOM ON A BUS IN INDIA

1

The Early Years (early 1980s)

Marriage is rarely trouble free, as anyone who has been married, even in the happiest of marriages, knows. Mom and I had our issues to work on (mostly me) like many other couples. However, every time our relationship hit some challenges, I said to myself, "I fell in love with her on a bus in India" and reflected on all those things I loved about Mom then that were still true. Our challenges always resolved themselves. I am biased, but I believe that Mom and I had an amazing love story that enriched both our lives, in many ways, and that led to our creating a wonderful family featuring you both. While it is tough to get over the fact that dear Mom's life was cut short by so many years, I know she lived a very rich life, richer than the lives of most people who will live thirty to forty years longer. Mom was blessed to live her early years with her loving family, Grandma Diane, Grandpa Lyell, Julie, and Brian. She had some incredible adventures with me. She gave and was the recipient of so much love from the friends she made, so easily, every place she went. And she gave birth to and raised the true loves of her life, the two of you.

It All Began at UC Irvine (1981)

My earliest recollection of Mom is the time she baked me and my college roommates a cake. I was living with my two best friends at UC Irvine (who remain very close friends today), Joe and Jeff. Though Mom and I were certainly friends, I don't remember being particularly close with her or why she baked us a cake. At that point, in the fall of 1981, Mom was a freshman at UC Irvine and I was a senior.

Joe, Jeff, and Barry (UC Irvine roommates and friends)

After Mom's gracious gesture, I remember that Joe, Jeff, and I decided to fix each other up for a dance at our fraternity, Beta Theta Pi. I chose to fix Joe up with Mom. Joe had no shortage of women who were interested in him in those days, and Jeff and I decided that it would be good for Joe to go out with someone with a much higher IQ than his average date had. Mom fit this description perfectly while also being cute and exceptionally kind.

It seemed as though Joe and Jeff felt the opposite about me, because they fixed me up with a high school senior who lived with her parents on Balboa Island, where we lived at 304 Collins Avenue. Joe, Jeff, and I and our dates had an incredibly fun evening. All six of us managed to squeeze into Joe's small VW bug. I remember hanging out with Joe and Jeff the next day, trying to rehash the events of the previous evening. Joe said, "Jackie was really fun. I tried to put the moves on her, but she gracefully slammed the door on that notion very quickly!"

Jackie and Leonore, UC Irvine, 1982

I honestly don't remember much about Mom or any interactions with her the rest of my senior year. Mom's "little sister" in her sorority, Leonore, said this about Mom during those years: "Jackie was effortlessly cool, incredibly funny, super pretty, and naturally charming. The real kicker for me was her authenticity and just how genuine and real she was. She was this warm blast of fresh, loving energy. We hit the ground running as friends. We were not terribly sorority-ish. We enjoyed the social aspect for sure, but both felt there was a big universe out there and wasted no time growing and learning more about the world. Jackie took the role of my big sister most seriously. One of her first tasks she felt was to teach me how to drive stick shift on her VW Rabbit. She simply could not let me go through life not knowing how to use a clutch and gears. No one knew how to host or entertain quite like Jackie. Much less when she was wrapping up at UCI in the later years and had that fantastic oceanfront home on the Balboa Peninsula with Wendy, Christine, and Stacy. Jackie even threw an elegant toga party there that everyone loved. Only she could pull off a classy toga party. We would head to the outskirts of Beverly Hills to a dance club called Odyssey. It was no alcohol and dancing only. She had this warmth, immediate ease, sense of humor, and connection. What an example she provided and set for me. At eighteen I was so incredibly impressed with her determination to stay authentic and true."

Mom's oldest friend, Mary, met her at the Marine Corps Air Station (MCAS) El Toro, California, where Mary's dad, General Richard Cooke, was the commander and where Grandpa had served earlier as commanding officer of the Marine Air Control Group 38. Mary was only one year behind Mom in school, and they stayed close friends when Mom went to UC Irvine. Mary noted: "Jackie lived at Newport Beach while I was a senior in high school. We would go down to her beach house and run around on the sand in the evenings and play Madonna songs and dance and have parties. We would also jump in her Rabbit and roam around Newport Beach, looking for fun parties, and eventually run into Ric Flores, and he would hang out with us and help us find fun parties to attend."

Ric, Mom's "big brother" in the Sigma Chi fraternity, also commented on how fun Mom was: "I remember a formal she invited me to (ONLY friends!) and said she'd pay for the rental of both our tuxedos (yes, she wore one too) if I'd pierce my ear. She took me to the mall and I still have the little cartilage in my lobe from that two-month period . . . a diamond no less!"

So many people have commented about how often Mom would bake something for someone, as she did for Joe, Jeff, and me when she baked us the cake. This practice extended to Mary's family as well: "Jackie was always baking chocolate chip cookies for my family. She loved baking and bringing over cookies and hanging out with my parents and talking and visiting with the whole family. She did it all the time! She would drive her brown Volkswagen Rabbit over the minute she knew she could come see us and bring cookies."

As for me, I was busy studying for my GMATs, applying to business schools, and planning a summer trip to Europe and a possible gap year before entering graduate school.

Becoming Close Friends (1985–1992)

In the early summer of 1982, only days after I graduated from college, I left for Europe, Israel, and Egypt, where I stayed for the next six months, deferring admission at both the UCLA and Columbia University graduate schools of business for one year. While I had been interested in business since early in college and knew I was destined to get my MBA, I felt that I was mentally unprepared for the rigors of graduate school academics and that I needed some adventure in my life. I certainly was not ready to make a choice between taking, in my mind, the comfortable way out and going to UCLA, which was close to home and which I knew well, or taking on the Big Apple and going to Columbia University.

Up until that point, I had backpacked in Western Europe twice, after high school at the age of eighteen with my friend Steve, and after my sophomore year in college at the age of twenty. After college, I was looking to up the level of adventure and was particularly interested in traveling to Egypt, Israel, and Turkey. After a few memorable weeks of travel in Turkey, partly inspired by *Midnight Express* (a movie I had seen a few years earlier, which features an American student sent to a Turkish prison for drug smuggling), I traveled all the way down through Egypt close to the border with Sudan. These trips stimulated in me a desire for further adventure, which became an important part of our early life together for Mom and me. Traveling to new places is something that really raises my spirits, particularly to those places less touched and influenced by Western culture. Being in Turkey at that time, even on a bus from Athens to Istanbul—an eighteen-hour journey—seemed very real, very authentic to me, as though I were in a real-life movie. I still remember meeting on the bus a very cute Italian girl, Loredana, who did not speak English. I did not yet speak Italian, so I communicated with her in Spanish. She told me that she was spending four days in Istanbul with her boyfriend but that he had enough money to fly there while she had to take the bus for lack of funds. That was not a chivalrous move on his part!

After Turkey, I took a series of boats across the Aegean and the Mediterranean Seas to Alexandria, Egypt, via Crete and Cyprus. I traveled almost the full length of Egypt by train and boat (along the Nile). I saw the pyramids of

Giza near Cairo and the Valley of the Kings near Luxor, relaxed in Aswan, and visited the massive rock temples of Abu Simbel, very close to the border with Sudan. What a great adventure! From Egypt, I traveled to Israel where I spent a few months. This was my first time in Israel. It was amazing exploring my roots, and I felt proud of my culture. I met relatives who had spent their whole lives on kibbutzim, even founding, for example, Kibbutz Ginosar in the Galilee. I do remember sending Mom a postcard from Israel that piqued her interest in the country, which we would all visit as a family a few times.

The other four months, before moving to New York in July of 1983, I worked in Los Angeles. I had, by then, broken up with my "kind-of" girlfriend and had made the decision to go to Columbia University instead of UCLA to get my MBA. I was excited about moving to New York to attend Columbia Graduate School of Business, but I was also a bit apprehensive. I was incredibly independent at a young age, but taking on the Big Apple necessitated even more independence in going outside my comfort zone. I remember arriving with my luggage by myself at Columbia, on the Upper West Side, near Harlem, at the age of twenty-three and going to the administrative office to secure my housing, only to be told that I would not get on-campus housing through the lottery but that off-campus housing services should be able to help. I had no place to sleep that night. I went to the house of the fraternity that I belonged to when I was at UC Irvine, Beta Theta Pi, and because it was still the end of summer, they were able to put me up for a week.

Finally, I found a tiny one-room studio in a building that Columbia owned. Nonstudents were still staying in the apartment building, and I was sharing a bathroom, down the hall, with a Pakistani family of five in the one-room apartment next door. I remember my friend Jeff coming to visit before I started school, and let's just say he left not a big fan of the area near Columbia.

While I was living in New York, Mom and I stayed in touch more regularly. After a successful summer internship with J.P. Morgan in the summer of 1984, I was offered a full-time job after graduating in 1985. I had decided to travel to South America after graduation from Columbia University. My intention was to travel overland from Argentina to California and then to New York to start my career. In fact, I did not even wait for graduation and was on a plane to Bue-

Jackie and Diane

nos Aires the day after my last final. I got lucky in making contact with some J.P. Morgan people in the Buenos Aires office, whom I met through my New York cousin Rita's sister and brother-in-law (Dorothy and Frank), who lived in Buenos Aires and seemed to know everyone.

The general manager, Tim Gibbs, offered me the opportunity to work in the J.P. Morgan office in Buenos Aires for four months before returning to New York to start the J.P. Morgan training program. I still got to travel a bit, to both Bolivia and Peru by train and bus, but the experience of working in Buenos Aires at such a young age (twenty-five) gave me the long-term vision of having an overseas career. Some of my Argentine colleagues in Buenos Aires would work directly with me throughout my career at J.P. Morgan, UBS, and ING-Barings for much of the next fifteen years. It was a tremendous experience to have my own apartment and job in Buenos Aires, a beautiful and fun city. I was lucky to have a number of Argentine colleagues as friends, which no doubt helped a lot with my Spanish. Just from that relatively short experience, even today when

I am in other Spanish-speaking countries, people ask if I have an Argentine background.

As for Mom, she spent two years at UC Irvine and then decided to take some time away from being a pre-med student to figure out what she wanted to do. She moved up from Orange County to San Francisco in 1984 and stayed for two years. This is where Mom met Vicki, who would become a lifelong friend and accompany her to India. As Grandpa and Grandma said, "Jackie talked to her dear friend, Vicki, about traveling, and Vicki agreed to go with her. They decided to go to India after being invited by our neighbor's mom who was visiting from there." But I am getting ahead of myself, as that trip would happen ten years later. Mom also used to see Vicki when she visited Orange County and Vicki went a few times to see Mom in Seattle. Vicki was such a loyal and good friend to Mom.

In the Bay Area, Mom worked for a film production company, Colossal Pictures, thinking she might want to work in the film industry. Given that we recently sold one of our vineyards to the Francis Ford Coppola Winery, it is ironic that dear Mom saved a bottle of wine that her boss at Colossal gave her—a bottle of 1983 Francis Ford Coppola Zinfandel. This was before Coppola even had a winery, and the wine was likely one of the first Coppola-labeled wines that he produced. When I would travel back to California from New York, I would go to the Bay Area and stay with my sister, Marci, where she lived in the Haight-Ashbury while attending Hastings Law School and then in Half Moon Bay in later years.

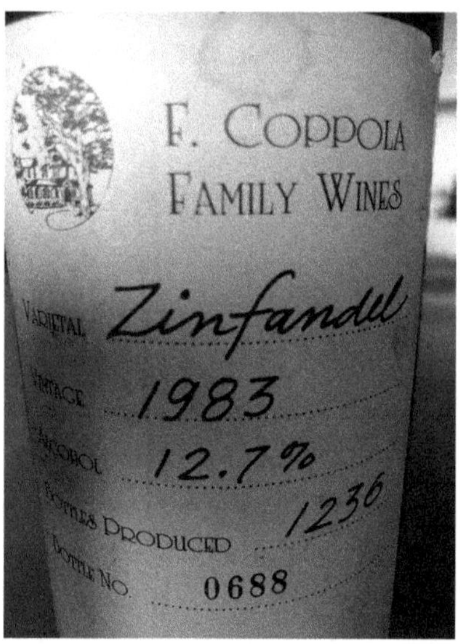

Coppola Wine, early years

On one of my trips to San Francisco, likely in 1984 or '85, I spent a really nice evening out with Mom, just as friends, and realized that I kind of liked her . . . her obvious beauty, kindness, and intelligence. More than anything, Mom was so easy to be around and her presence always lifted my spirits! On another trip back from New York, I went to Palm Springs and stayed at our condo at the Racquet Club. Mom came to visit, as did my close friend from high school, Patty, and her boyfriend Gary. After that, I suggested that Mom should come out to New York to visit me. Although I don't remember exactly what I was feeling, I knew that I was attracted to Mom and also liked her a lot as a friend. While I stayed friends with many women from high school (who are still close friends today), Mom was the only woman I stayed in touch with from UC Irvine. At one point, I had tried to plant a kiss on Mom when I saw her in San Francisco, which she deftly rejected because she had a serious boyfriend then. It certainly added to the already great respect I had for Mom. As Mom said, "Part of me always liked Barry, but the timing was never right."

In those days, because of my great experience with J.P. Morgan in Buenos Aires and my continuing effort to improve my Spanish, I hung out almost exclusively with Latinos in New York. My best friend at J.P. Morgan at the time, Manuel, was from Guatemala, and during Christmas and New Year's in 1986, I traveled there and stayed with his family, as well as traveling to Honduras and El Salvador. I remember sending Mom a postcard from El Salvador. She thought I was crazy to travel there. In those years right-wing paramilitary death squads were waging a surrogate war across much of Central America with support from the United States, which feared that communism would sweep through the region after Nicaragua became communist. I enjoyed taking a class in Central American affairs and reading *Inevitable Revolutions* by Walter LaFeber when the Iran-Contra affair during the Reagan administration was exposed. I was definitely a "lefty" in college.

Whenever I was in touch with Mom, she would always ask about my travels, not out of courtesy but sincerely, because they probably intrigued her. Shortly thereafter, she told me on the phone (believe it or not, there was no such thing as email or texting then) that she was taking me up on my suggestion to visit me in New York.

That visit took place in 1986. By that time I was working on Wall Street for J.P. Morgan, and it was shortly before I left the United States in the summer of 1987 for Paris, not to return to live in the United States permanently until 2002.

I remember being very excited about Mom's visit. I purchased two tickets to *Cats*, the Broadway musical, and arranged to get Mom on the floor of the stock exchange. This is where one of Mom's top five stories comes into play: she called me from the airport, from a pay phone, to tell me that she had arrived, that she "kind of" had a boyfriend, Mark, and that he was "kind of" on the same flight to New York but had "definitely" arranged his own accommodations. Once in Manhattan, Mom then followed up with a second phone call to let me know that his accommodations had "kind of" fallen through and to ask if he could also stay with me. I am not sure why, but without much thought, I readily agreed to this definitely out-of-the-ordinary request. The result was that the three of us stayed in my tiny one-bedroom apartment on 69th between Columbus and Central Park West. Did I not really care? Was I trying to impress Mom by being so easygoing? Was it for the future story value of this strange episode? This story did become no. 1 of all of Mom's stories, which she usually told within minutes of our meeting new people. Mark did leave a few days early, so I had Mom a bit to myself to meet with some friends, take her to *Cats*, and do some other fun things. I learned only recently, on Yom Kippur, 2018, from reading Mom's diary that she was interested in me as more than just a friend while in NYC. I was obviously interested in her as more than just a friend, but I was also content just to be her friend. Mom wrote: "Once I came to visit him when he was in New York, and my boyfriend at the time, Mark, ended up staying with him. Mark left for England, and I stayed on in New York. I was sitting next to Barry one night in his apartment in New York after Mark left. We were reading something together or looking at photographs. I remember wanting to kiss him then. . . . I had this pleasant sensation sitting next to him."

In the summer of 1987, J.P. Morgan transferred me to Paris. The company enjoyed a very privileged position in France as the following excerpt from the J.P. Morgan website makes clear: "J.P. Morgan claimed its place in the history of La République when it made a loan of £10m to Napoleon III. Napoleon used this loan to launch the Franco-Prussian war of 1870–1871. The war led to the surrender of the Alsace region to Germany, but confirmed J.P. Morgan as a friend of the French government. In return, the bank was gifted a building

J.P. Morgan Paris, Place Vendôme

in Paris's Place de la Concorde, which it swapped in 1916 for its current office in Place Vendôme."

Paris had been my dream posting since I started at J.P. Morgan, and I had been studying French on the remote possibility of getting that coveted transfer. While I loved working for J.P. Morgan, made lifelong friends there, and was really stimulated by the work, my no. 1 goal was always to work overseas, and I was very lucky to get a plum assignment in the Paris office so early in my career. I thank my mentor, Marcus Meier, for bringing me to Paris. He was also personally responsible for sending me to Tokyo, Singapore, and Zurich. I learned much from him, and not just about the financial markets but about people and life.

That move launched me, and then our family, on a series of international moves (to seven countries, with two moves to Singapore and two to London, thus nine international moves). I remember Mom telling me that on a winter ski trip to Austria with her family, she stopped in Paris, in 1987, with her boyfriend, Mark, and wanted to see me, but Mark refused. Shortly after that, Mom wrote to tell me that she had broken up with Mark and had also made the decision to return to UCI to finish getting her degree in biology. Mom's roommate when she returned to UCI, Karen, wrote that "Jackie loved to take power walks around the island to take a break from studying. We would walk often especially during finals. She was always focused on health and she was a very healthy eater which is common for people now but not at that time. She was a thoughtful person who loved surprising people and giving gifts." Mom was also a very determined student, particularly after going back to college, as Karen noted: "We used to study together in the basement of the library at UC Irvine. Jackie was a serious student. Her love of animals was apparent even in college. There was a stray dark gray cat that she loved and fed where we lived on Balboa Island at 310 Onyx."

Mom graduated from UCI in 1990 and shortly thereafter moved up north to Seattle, where she met another lifelong very close friend, another Karen. Mom spent the next couple of years in Seattle and a few months living on San Juan Island, which we visited as a family around 2012. As Karen noted: "I met Jackie in '89 or '90 through my boyfriend Eugene, who was working on his PhD along with friends of Jackie's and others in the genetics labs. We did almost all our socializing in big groups of people associated with the labs. I loved her from day one. She was bright and cheerful and even back then always brought gifts to every occasion where she was a guest. Flowers or chocolates usually." Mom and Karen shared a very special friendship for many years!

Home
Menu
Location
Gallery
Reviews
About Us
Order Online
Palace
2424 Van Ness Ave, San Francisco, CA 94109
(415) 345-0072
PALACE
11/23/94
Singapore:
I am sitting in Barry's house at his
dining room table. Downstairs, the floors
SINGAPORE 75c
Pin cushion star
SINGAPORE
Thanksgiving in Las Vegas... maybe you'll have something to really be thankful about... like winning lots of $$!
Love,
Lyell + Diane Holmes
5 FALLING LEAF
IRVINE, CA 92715
U. S. A.
8 888498 744451
Distributed by: ASSOCIATED MARKETING AGENCY PTE. LTD.

2

In Singapore and India: Traveling and Falling in Love (November 1994)

That next year, toward the end of 1988, I was transferred to J.P. Morgan's Tokyo office. I went kicking and screaming. I had the ideal life, working for a great company, speaking French every day, in perhaps the world's most beautiful city, Paris, with a great social network of French friends.

The then head of the J.P. Morgan office in Paris, Marcus Meier, was transferred to run the Tokyo office and had asked me to move there. What really made the decision for me was that Marcus was, by far, the best boss I ever had. He was a self-made Swiss man who was wicked smart, very tough, and very fair, and he really wanted to develop his close staff, challenge them, and bring out their best qualities. He had some very rare managerial traits that I have tried to emulate during my own career.

I really did not want to go to Tokyo. Up until then I never really had much interest in Asia. However, I finally succumbed, realizing that it would be an interesting adventure and good for my career, both of which proved true. As Steve Jobs said, "You can only connect the dots afterwards."

Although I did choose my career over my happiness on that occasion, there was a direct connection between my moving to Asia and getting together with Mom. Moreover, I was fascinated by Japanese culture, particularly in the work environment, and became very close with a number of J.P. Morgan Japanese staff, one of whom, Yo Nakagawa, I still count as a close friend. I managed a group of about ten staff at J.P. Morgan Tokyo, and we regularly did things together, even on weekends. This gave me keen insight directly into the Japanese culture, a culture for which I have great respect.

Barry waterskiing, Singapore, 1990

After only one year working in Tokyo, I was transferred in 1990 to Singapore. By then, I had begun a relationship with a close friend from high school, and she had moved to Singapore to be with me. I was very involved with my career at that point and that came first. In addition, I was likely not mature enough emotionally to be in a serious relationship at that time. As I was to blame for not putting enough effort into the relationship, she moved back to the US.

As you know, I loved living in Singapore in those early years, 1990 to '92. I had a great job, a great lifestyle, and an amazing group of colleagues who were also (and still are) close friends. I owned a ski boat with Yo, Mike, and Roy, and we went out waterskiing practically every weekend, often with my friend Siu Mei as well. We would regularly eat on Pulau Ubin, a small nondescript island where the most amazingly fresh and tasty seafood was served in a very basic outdoor setting.

One weekend day, only my friend Don could go skiing. We were cruising down a nearby Malaysian river. I was driving the boat and he was skiing. I looked back and saw something that looked like a big log in the water. As I passed it and before Don caught up with it, I realized that it was a crocodile with its mouth open! I yelled to Don, "Don't fall, mate," pointed down, and made a gesture with my arms to indicate a croc. We did other fun things like weekend scuba-diving trips to a nearby chain of Malaysian islands.

In 1992, I remember Mom sending me an invitation to her first wedding (and even sending me photos of the wedding later). Unfortunately, I was unable to attend. Less than two years later, Mom contacted me again, saying that she was passing through Singapore on her way to India after a difficult breakup with her ex-husband. At that point, I had no idea how devastated Mom was about the way her breakup came about. She would be traveling with her friend Vicki. I invited them to come stay with me in Singapore but mentioned that I was on the move as well.

After ten years with J.P. Morgan, I decided to take a one-year sabbatical away from finance and go to China to continue my Mandarin-language studies. Before Mom and Vicki left for Singapore (on the way to India), I had a planned trip back to Sausalito, where I had purchased a house in 1991, to drop off some of my stuff in advance of my move out of Singapore. Mom drove up to Sausalito to spend a few days with me. It was great spending time with Mom, particularly in Sausalito. There was something so special for me about Sausalito, its small-town nature in the evening, the many tourists speaking all kinds of languages during the day, the beautiful water views, and the nature in the hills above that goes for miles.

Golden Gate Bridge

Mom and I took some nice walks around Sausalito and talked a lot, as she was

Helmand Palace, San Francisco, 1994

still quite sad about the breakup of her marriage. She had some healing to do. I remember her taking me to the Afghan restaurant Helmand Palace in the city and thinking how cool it was that, out of all the places Mom could choose to take me, it was an Afghan restaurant. It is apparently owned by the brother of Hamid Karzai, the first president of Afghanistan, and is also the place where we had our first date (at least that is the way I see it), though we were only friends then. I would host a surprise fifteenth anniversary dinner for Mom with many of our friends at this restaurant in February of 2012.

We had such a nice dinner and conversation. I definitely found Mom attractive and really enjoyed her company, but I also knew that she had just gone through a difficult end to her short marriage. I thought it might be better

Jackie at a "hawker stand," Singapore, 1994

On Sentosa Island, Singapore, 1994

Children in Kashgar, China, Central Asia, 1993

being her close friend than working on something more than that and risk our friendship if it did not work out. I was likely overthinking things.

After Mom's November 1994 visit to Sausalito, she returned home to Southern California to get ready for her trip to India, and I returned to Singapore. Mom and Vicki arrived in Singapore a few weeks later. I showed them around and remember going to a bar, having a few too many drinks, and singing karaoke. Mom absolutely hated karaoke but was always a good sport! Mom and Vicki remained in my house in Singapore for a few more days while I returned, again, to the Bay Area to have Thanksgiving dinner with Marci and Uncle Brian, Baba Toba, and others. Mom wrote in her diary on November 23, 1994: "I am sitting in Barry's house at his dining room table. Downstairs, the floors are marble. Upstairs, they are wood. The house is beautiful and he has filled it with Asian relics that describe the past several years of his life in the East. On the walls, he has hung photographs of his journeys through China . . . all of the pho-

Jackie and Barry, Raffles Bar, Singapore, 1994

tographs are of people . . . most of them children . . . and they look as if a photographer from National Geographic took them. In front of me is one of four children, sitting together on a bench. The background is grey cobblestone. Three of the children are dressed in shades of red, magenta, orange. The other child is in tan and is the only one looking into the camera. Their ethnicity seems to be Moslem. It is a wonderful photograph as are the others that adorn the walls.

"As I look around this place, I am realizing why people have children. . . . Barry should have a child because someday that child would look over these photographs that his father had taken and realize the richness in this man's life . . . the adventures he has had and the genuine love he possessed for Asia. He is not consumed by it, but it does border on passion. I envy Barry AND I love him dearly. He left this morning for the States to visit his family. I miss him very much. In my heart, I never want Barry to marry anyone. . . . But I would make an exception for Vicki . . . or MYSELF!"

This was vintage Mom, totally willing to offer a guy she apparently liked to her close friend (whether or not her close friend was interested). Vicki has really been an amazing friend to Mom, as was her friend from Seattle, Karen. Mom loved them both! Again, I was attracted to Mom and enjoyed her company a lot. I loved her sense of humor, her intelligence, her kindness and beauty. But I really was not ready to rush into a relationship. At times, I even felt that I might never be ready for a real relationship at all. I had been so independent from such a young age, had moved around so much, and had already had one relationship with a close friend that did not work out. I knew I had a lot to learn on this topic of relationships and was not sure I had it in me to do the work necessary to have a positive relationship experience.

I had a particularly great job during my second time around in Singapore (my first stint in Singapore was from 1990 to '92, the second from 1993 to '95, with a year in Zurich in between) with J.P. Morgan and was very well compensated. I got the opportunity to start a new business, Asia Local Emerging Markets, with a big team of people from a number of Asian countries and staff in Hong Kong, Bombay, Indonesia, and the Philippines, as well as Singapore.

My team did stuff together all the time. A favorite was at end of the month when we would all go to the running track, run one mile together, and then go out for dinner. If our financial results were good for the month, on budget or better, I would pay for the group's dinner. However, because we were in Asia where so many things entail placing a bet, we placed bets on our times in running the mile, with the caveat that the running times were handicapped.

For example, if one runner ran the mile in exactly six minutes and the other runner in seven minutes, then the slower runner has a minus-one-minute handicap. We would place bets on each other. It was a very fun bonding experience. I also had a great group of friends, mostly J.P. Morgan colleagues.

Despite this, something was missing in my life, and this was part of the reason for my taking a sabbatical. In hindsight, while I don't necessarily believe in fate, I do think that stepping off the workaholic track with J.P. Morgan gave me the time, mental state, and space to be in a position to develop a relationship with Mom. For this, I am incredibly grateful that I took that fork in the road and can, today, "connect those dots." Still, at that point, spending time with Mom in

WELCOME TO SINGAPORE
Spectacular view of Chinese Garden during mid-Autumn Festival.

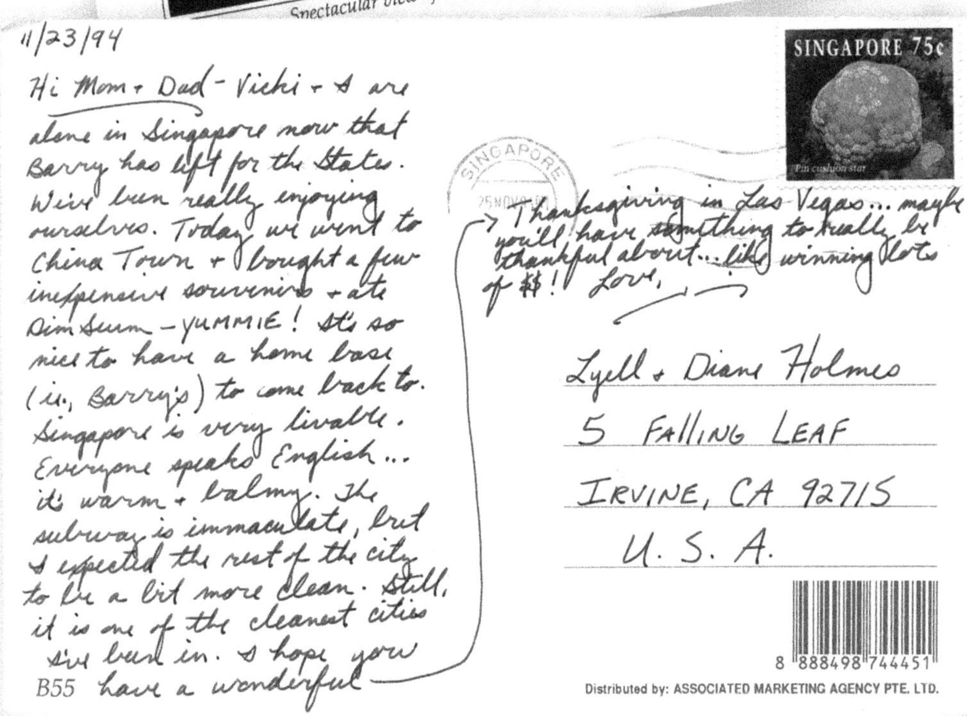
11/23/94

Hi Mom + Dad - Vicki + I are alone in Singapore now that Barry has left for the States. We've been really enjoying ourselves. Today we went to China Town + bought a few inexpensive souvenirs + ate Dim Sum - YUMMIE! It's so nice to have a home base (i.e., Barry's) to come back to. Singapore is very livable. Everyone speaks English... it's warm + balmy. The subway is immaculate, but I expected the rest of the city to be a bit more clean. Still, it is one of the cleanest cities I've been in. I hope you have a wonderful Thanksgiving in Las Vegas... maybe you'll have something to really be thankful about... like winning lots of $$! Love,

B55

SINGAPORE 75c
Pin cushion star

SINGAPORE 25 NOV 94

Lyell + Diane Holmes
5 FALLING LEAF
IRVINE, CA 92715
U. S. A.

8 888498 744451

Distributed by: ASSOCIATED MARKETING AGENCY PTE. LTD.

A postcard from Singapore, 1994

INDIA
1. DEHLI
2. KASHMIR, SRINAGAR
3. DHARAMSALA
4. AGRA
5. PUSHKAR

BURMA
6. YANGON
7. MANDALAY
8. BAGAN

THAILAND
9. BANGKOK
10. KOH SAMUI

LAOS
11. VIENTIANE
12. LUANG PRABANG
13. BOTEN

CHINA
14. KUNMING
15. BEIJING

SINGAPORE
16. SINGAPORE

Singapore, I was not really thinking about a long-term, or even short-term, future with her. I was enjoying the moment. On November 23, 1994, Mom sent a postcard to Grandma and Grandpa, writing: "Vicki and I are alone in Singapore now that Barry has gone to the States. We've been really enjoying ourselves. Today we went to China Town and bought a few inexpensive souvenirs and ate dim sum—YUMMIE! It's so nice to have a home base (i.e., Barry's) to come back to. Singapore is very livable. Everyone speaks English . . . it's warm and balmy. The subway is immaculate, but I expected the rest of the city to be a bit cleaner. Still, it is one of the cleanest cities I've ever been in. I hope you have a wonderful Thanksgiving in Las Vegas . . . maybe you'll have something to really be thankful about . . . like winning lots of $$! Love, Jackie."

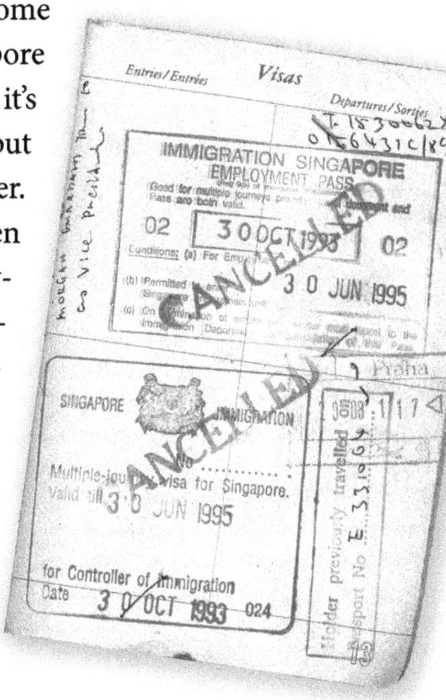

By the time I returned to Singapore, in early December of 1994, Mom and Vicki had left for India. I had decided that I would spend a few weeks traveling with them in India before heading to China to start my sabbatical. Why was I going to India? I had been in India many times, as the business I ran at J.P. Morgan had a joint-venture with India's largest bank, ICICI, and the unit I ran in Singapore, Asia Local Emerging Markets, was responsible for training its financial markets staff. I spent at least a couple of days in Bombay every few months for about a year and a half. Was I going to India to hang out with Mom and Vicki? Did I really want to go to India, before heading to China? Or was I intrigued with the prospect of being around Mom and possibly, finally, getting together with her?

I am not sure of the answer to these questions even today. Mom wrote in her diary, "We arrived in the New Delhi train terminal and took a rickshaw to the YMCA International Guest House. Our room had the best shower in all of

Vicki and Jackie in a rickshaw in Benares, India, 1994

India . . . HOT water and great force. I was really looking forward to seeing Barry but not so hot about seeing Delhi."

Mom wrote of the area around the mosque in Old Delhi: "I noticed there was a group of 10 young males up ahead sitting watching us and absolutely no females, except for Vicki and me. I said, 'I don't think this is a good idea.' And when we turned to walk away they started verbally taunting us. One man grabbed my arm and I said, 'get away.' I had such an impulse to punch his face. We quickly got a rickshaw back to the hotel."

I remember arriving in the middle of the night in Delhi and going to meet Mom and Vicki at their hotel. There was something very weird with the taxi driver, and at a stopping place, where other taxis were parked, I ordered him to stop. I got out of the taxi and into a different one. In hindsight, I was surely being set up for some kind of robbery. I was in a new place and it was the middle of the night. It was not an auspicious way to start my sabbatical. I was sure happy to see Mom and Vicki.

Mom wrote: "Barry arrived at about 4:00 in the morning and Vicki and I were *so glad* . . . a westernized, civilized male." We spent a day or two in Delhi. I took them out to what I still think is one of the best meals I ever had, at an Indian restaurant, Bukhara, in the Sheraton Hotel. Mom wrote: "The driver took me and Vicki to the Sheraton Hotel where we met up with Barry for dinner and what a dinner . . . it was *sublime*!"

We had decided to travel up north to Kashmir, then Dharamsala (where the Dalai Lama lived) before going to Rajasthan. I would then leave them for China, Vicki would go home, and Mom would go back to Bangalore where she would be doing a science-based internship at an institute. After traveling with Mom for a few days and thinking about her, I recalled the description of a woman with a "nice aura" made by a Japanese guy who worked for me at the J.P. Morgan Tokyo office, Ken Katsumata. One day he asked to meet with me and said, "Barry-san, I want you to know that I want to go out with Honda-san." Honda-san was a woman who worked at the opposite desk in the office. I asked, "Katsumata-san, why do you want to go out with her?" His response aptly described exactly why I liked being around Mom: "Because, Barry-san, she has a *nice atmosphere*!"

TAJ MAHAL
IND
100
भारत INDIA
500
LYELL + DIANE H
5 FALLING LEAF
IRVINE, CA
92715
U.S.A.
722. © Lustre Press, 4 Ansari Road, Delhi.
night — this marble mausoleum is at its most bewitching when seen on a full moon's night.
2.00 भारत INDIA

3

Our India Adventure Begins (December 1994)

We flew over the Himalayas to get to Kashmir. What used to be one of the most popular tourist destinations was devoid of tourists because of the conflict between India and Pakistan over the area. It did not help that it was the middle of winter high up in the Himalayas and freezing cold. Mom wrote of our idea to go to Kashmir: "An Indian woman asked me why I was going to Kashmir. I said, 'Because it was recommended and beautiful.' She said, 'Yes, it is beautiful, but it is dangerous now. I can't understand why you would go there with all the other beautiful places to visit in India. May God be with you.'"

While I did not necessarily feel a sense of responsibility for Mom and Vicki, although that would definitely change with Mom later, I was careful not to force my sense of adventure on them. I did realize that going to Kashmir, in those days and at that time of year, was maybe not the best idea, but it was also a place I had dreamed of going to.

We stayed in one of the famous houseboats in Srinagar. It was lovely and, despite no other tourists being around, we had a great time. I remember almost burning the houseboat down while trying to toss an overheated log from the furnace into the lake where the houseboat was. I eventually did toss the burning log into the lake but also the big metal tongs used to grab the log. We all laughed so hard that Mom actually peed in her pants.

Mom wrote of the houseboat: "The houseboat is elaborately carved with lotus flowers, peacocks, etc. all out of cedar. It smells wonderful. It is peaceful here, on the water . . . a welcome change from Delhi. I am sitting outside here on the houseboat, writing and listening to the few sounds here . . . a man in

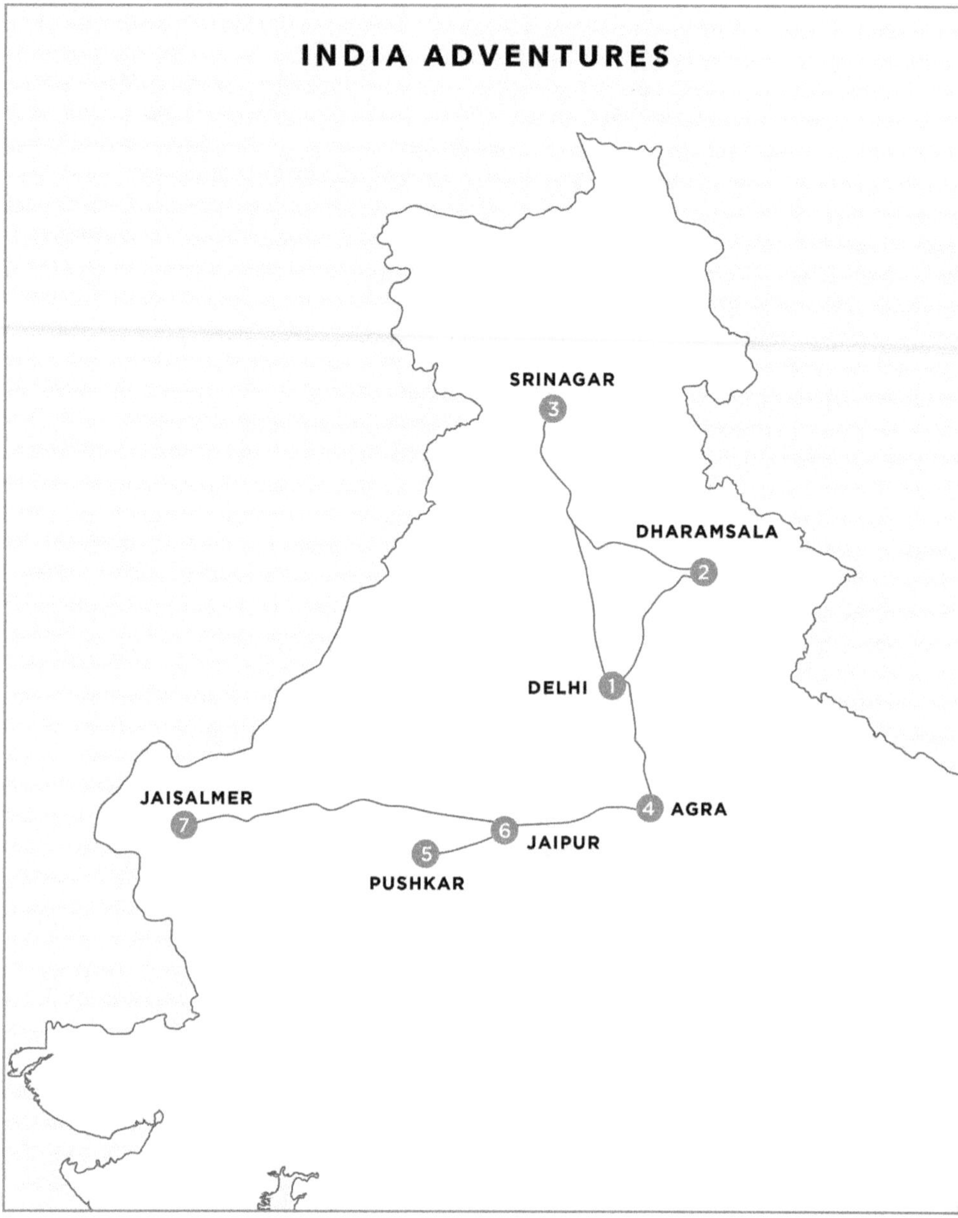
INDIA ADVENTURES
SRINAGAR
3
DHARAMSALA
2
DELHI
1
JAISALMER
7
4
AGRA
6
JAIPUR
5
PUSHKAR

Jackie and Vicki in Srinagar, Kashmir, India, 1994

adjacent houseboat humming . . . a crow calling, Vicki sniffling . . . water. It is beautiful here."

Mom was relatively new to overseas traveling. Her only overseas experiences were a winter family trip to Austria while she was in college and a trip or two to England. I loved how at ease she was in some very exotic, distant, and materially poor places. She always seemed to pick out and describe beauty so accurately and vividly. She treated everyone she met with kindness and dignity. Mom was so positive and interested in everything, and it was just another one, on a list of many things, that I loved about her. She was so often in the "flow" of our traveling experience and, in that respect, we were in sync. I could not possibly have imagined a better travel partner.

However, we noticed that Vicki's mood was not as buoyant as it had been, likely due to the hard travel, the tough conditions, and some aggressive people we would often have to deal with during bus travel. One day we got a guide to

On a houseboat, Srinagar, Kashmir, India, 1994

drive us up to the higher elevations of the Himalayas. Mom wrote: "We passed through villages and snow and cold. We stopped at a village at the base of a mountain and got on these small horses with very long hair. There were many children . . . all boys but very friendly. People smiled at us here. It was snowing throughout our trek. We passed many army checkpoints with hundreds of Indian soldiers around."

After a few days in Kashmir, we made our way to McLeod Ganj, Dharamsala, where the Dalai Lama lives. It was a long journey from Kashmir to Dharamsala, as Mom wrote: "We've spent the last two days on a bus. The bus from Srinagar to Jammu was a bit harrowing at times, twisting, snowy roads throughout the mountains."

Our first day in Dharamsala was on Christmas Day 1994. Mom wrote: "It is Christmas. Barry, Vicki and I are sitting in a very small café in McLeod Ganj of Dharamsala. It is quite cold, but the sun has come out and has begun to thaw our icy bones. From the window, we can see a family of macaques on the aluminum rooftop below us. McLeod Ganj is set high in the hills with narrow curvy streets and pine trees all around and a lot of Tibetan Monks walking all around with their shaved heads and burgundy and pink robes . . . oh yes, and macaques everywhere."

Mom continued in her diary the next day, December 26, 1994: "Barry and I took a walk around the little town here and visited a Buddhist temple and went in search of the Dalai Lama's residence. The Dalai Lama's presence here is notable. McLeod Ganj is lovely. I am so glad we came. I have decided to travel to Vietnam with Barry and perhaps to China, if he can tolerate me for that long." Then on December 27, she wrote: "Before I launch into Agra, a few more words about Dharamsala/McLeod Ganj. First of all, on 12/27 Barry saw the Dalai Lama at the Buddhist temple. It was inspiring for him. Before that, Barry and I were caught in a short storm blast and sought out refuge inside a small restaurant/café . . . the one we had eaten breakfast in the previous day. McLeod Ganj has several of these wonderful rustic cafés . . . great for hanging out in and reading or writing postcards, etc. I am reluctant to leave this place. . . . There is something here that clears the mind and leaves it open for reflection and thought in general."

Tibetan Buddhist monks in training, McLeod Ganj, India, 1994

I had, by then, developed feelings for Mom, though I was likely pushing them away, possibly due to feeling vulnerable about expressing my interest in her, but it was in McLeod Ganj that I started to be continually conscious of her presence and its very positive impact on me. It is likely that being in such a sacred place, with many Tibetan refugees, Tibetan monasteries, the home of the Dalai Lama (and his presence all over the town), and the ubiquitous coffee shops that often triggered meaningful conversations with the many foreigners we met, led me to serious reflection on my feelings for Mom. I am not sure if I knew it consciously then, but clearly I was falling in love with her.

Despite enjoying Dharamsala, I was looking forward to going to Agra to see the famous Taj Mahal and then on to Rajasthan. While I had developed very strong feelings for Mom the previous week, I was quite sure she was not aware of where my head was at. We were still just friends.

The next few days, in Agra, at the Taj Mahal, would change my life forever (and yours as well) in the best possible way. As I have told the story before,

Jackie in India, 1994

it was on the night bus from Dharamsala to Agra that I sat up a good part of the night watching Mom while she slept and realizing consciously, for the first time, that I was very much in love with her. I already knew her well, we got along great, and I was very much attracted to her stunning beauty, and there was great chemistry between us. I loved Mom's "atmosphere." I even can vividly remember the jacket she was wearing on the bus and the red scarf around her neck. I don't know what came over me while looking at her on the bus ride at night, but it was a strong gravitational pull that is very hard to describe. By the next morning, still a day or two before we would both express our love for each other, everything felt right in the world and I knew my life was changed, for the better, forever . . . and indeed it was. I think about that bus ride all the time and frequently included that memory in cards (particularly for our anniversaries). It was one brief moment in time, easily identifiable, easily remembered, and that gives me great comfort, especially these days. I feel blessed to be able to say

Jackie at the Taj Mahal . . . "I fell in love with your mom on a bus in India," 1994

that "I fell in love with your mom on a bus in India!" We arrived in Agra, and Vicki, Mom, and I visited the Taj Mahal the next morning. What an amazing work of art, an absolute treasure, definitely one of the top five most beautiful places I have seen. I remember that Vicki decided to go back to our hotel because she was not feeling well. And this may be TMI for you both, but it was at the Taj Mahal where I told Mom that I liked her, we kissed, and from then onward we were together.

The date was December 28, 1994. By then, Mom had been firmly in my consciousness since she and Vicki visited me in Singapore, and I had been traveling with her nonstop for roughly ten days. As dear Mom wrote: "And now we are in Agra and getting ready to leave tomorrow for Rajasthan. The Taj Mahal is Beauty and Devotion incarnate, so to speak. And truly magnificent. The entire mausoleum is in marble, and around the two tombs is an elaborately carved

A postcard from the Taj Mahal, 1994

lattice with inlaid stone of lotus flowers, etc. It was amazing." Mom continued: "Barry, Vicki and I lay on the grass in front of the Taj . . . the area around it was beautifully landscaped and clean. Vicki went back to the hotel because she had a bad headache and left Barry and me alone on the lawn."

I will save you guys from the rest of Mom's entry, but from that moment on, at the Taj Mahal, Mom and I became a couple in love. Mom wrote: "I care for Barry deeply. I hope all goes well for the rest of our journeys together. Tomorrow, on to Rajasthan." I felt the same for Mom— and not just the way you feel when you meet someone new that you like, and your heart skips a beat. This was different. It was like I knew that I had put in place a very important piece that was missing from the puzzle of my life.

The next day, December 30, Mom wrote a postcard to Grandma and Grandpa that read: "Dear Mom and Dad . . . I apologize for my handwriting, but I'm writing this in a car . . . we're on our way to Pushkar in Rajasthan from Agra home to the Taj Mahal. The Taj Mahal is SPECTACULARLY BEAUTIFUL. Barry, I and Vicki have been having a wonderful time. We loved Kashmir and Dharamsala. I'll write a letter with more detail, but for now I just wanted to let you know that I'm doing fine and I'm very sorry I didn't get a chance to talk with you on Christmas or your birthday, Mom. I hope both were joyous and merry. I also apologize for the lack of presents to open for Christmas . . . but I do have some nice things for the two of you . . . we'll have to have another Christmas when I get back . . . which brings me to the real intent of this note . . . being, 'when I get back' . . . Barry has made me an offer I can't refuse, which is to 'sponsor' me as his travel companion through Asia. I'll meet him in Bangkok shortly and from there go with him to Vietnam and China. I've decided to do this instead of working in Bangalore. We'll travel together until a) I get sick of him, b) he gets sick of me, or c) I get too homesick to bear. I'm very excited about our travel plans, as I think it will be a fabulous experience. I'm not sure how long our journey will take, but I'll keep you posted. I miss you both very much and am looking forward to seeing my wonderful family and telling you all about my travels. How is little Gryphen? I miss her terribly at times, especially whenever I see another dog. Take care! Love, Jackie."

Of that time Grandma and Grandpa noted: "Of course we were concerned and wondered, hoped that Jackie was safe, healthy and happy in countries we knew very little about. We never really knew exactly where she was until we received a letter. There was no internet or cell phones in those days. When we did hear from her we relaxed, smiled and said, 'Thank God she is OK!'"

As for me, it was strange, at that point, being good friends with Mom for fourteen years, getting invited to her first wedding, becoming very close to her since Mom and Vicki were in Singapore in November, and now being in love with her but never having met her parents. As Lyell and Diane said: "We initially wondered about her traveling companion, Barry, not ever having met him. But we took comfort in knowing our daughter, Jackie, and the foundation we laid for her. We were confident she was with someone who was respectful, considerate, caring, helpful, and kind to her." Mom always spoke glowingly about Grandma Diane and Grandpa Lyell and what a great childhood she had growing up with them and her siblings, Julie and Brian. I knew they had been very concerned about Mom after her marriage dissolved and was not sure exactly what they thought of her traipsing around Asia with some old college friend. In addition, Grandpa had been a colonel in the Marines, and he and Grandma were devout Catholics while I was Jewish and had never met anyone in the military before.

Some tension was building, though, with Vicki. In hindsight, she may have reached critical mass with some of the challenges many deal with in traveling through India. Jackie wrote: "The past few days have been somewhat tense, as I felt that Vicki was slipping into a foul mood . . . deeper and deeper. Finally, yesterday afternoon in the car when we arrived in Jaipur, Vicki seemed to snap a bit at something I said, and Barry turned around and said, 'Vicki for the last two days you have been the moodiest fucking person I have ever met in my life!'"

About that terrible comment I made, Mom wrote: "Vicki was totally caught off guard and my heart plummeted into my gut." I still regret that comment to this day and have told Vicki this many times, as Vicki loved Mom so much and was one of her best, oldest, and most loyal friends. Mom also loved Vicki immensely and I had messed up. Vicki did not deserve that outburst. I knew I had gone too far, but in hindsight I think part of it was a protective shield I had developed for Mom, which was my issue. Mom was right when she wrote: "I felt that Barry's comment to Vicki was very unnecessary and I was angry. The rest of the car ride to Pushkar was a blur. Vicki was quite comatose. Barry said nothing. I hate conflict."

Things did get better over the next few days, but I did feel bad for snapping at Vicki and even more for the difficult position I had put Mom in. It was a bad mistake that I regretted! Here is Mom's diary entry for December 31, 1994, from Pushkar, India: "The last day of 1994. Pushkar is a wonderful place. The buildings are all white-washed and set around a lake. . . . It is much more relaxed, much less crowded and lovely. We switched hotels and are thrilled to be at the Pushkar Palace Hotel now. Our room is beautiful and very clean. Two of our windows have a view of the lake. The grounds have green grass and rose

Pushkar, India, 1994

bushes and trees . . . very lush . . . wicker chairs and marble tables. The porters and door guards are dressed in white with bright turbans and long curling mustaches."

As Vicki was leaving soon to return to California, we decided on January 1, 1995, that Mom and Vicki would go back to Bangalore (remember that Mom had originally planned to spend six months in Bangalore working in a lab, but, thankfully for you guys and me, decided to abandon those plans and travel with me to China) to get their stuff and I would travel by myself farther into Rajasthan and then on to Delhi to meet Mom. Mom wrote in her diary about the restaurant where we ate our New Year's dinner: "I picked the Rainbow Rooftop Restaurant and took responsibility for the outcome. The food was great and they had everything from lasagna to hummus to falafels. But the highlight of the meal was the 'Special Lassies' that they served. The owner suggested it; 'You can try my special lassie made with bananas and marijuana . . . very good,' he announced. Vicki decided to try it and ended up completely stoned by the end of the evening. . . . It was hysterical." The next day, Mom and Vicki returned to Bangalore where they had started their trip. Mom would see Vicki off back to the US, and I traveled deeper into Rajasthan, to Jaisalmer, which was fascinating. My guidebook mentioned that "Jaisalmer is a former medieval trading center in the Western Indian state of Rajasthan in the heart of the Thar Desert. It is dominated by the huge and impressive Jaisalmer Fort and also the Maharaja's Palace with intricately carved Jain temples."

At that point, Mom and I had been traveling together for two weeks and had declared our love for each other for barely a week, so it was strange to be apart from her. Certainly, the excitement and adventure of a new place was great, but I missed Mom by my side. Being so independent and having lived and traveled a lot by myself, it was a new sensation for me to miss someone, and that reaffirmed my decision to ask Mom to travel with me.

Mom's entry, from Bangkok, Thailand, for January 8, 1995: "I'm flying to Delhi to meet Barry. This is my fifth trip to Delhi and I don't even like Delhi . . . but it is a hub and there is a Burmese Embassy there, and I do need a visa to Burma where Barry and I are planning to go." Mom continued: "Today, we are leaving India. I am happy to be leaving Delhi, but I am not ready to leave the rest of this country behind which is exactly how I like to depart from somewhere . . . with the intention of returning. I must come back to India some time, and spend more time in Rajasthan . . . and Kerala. I'm off to Bangkok now with Barry." Unfortunately, neither Mom nor I was to return to India.

Mom's entry from Bangkok on January 12, 1995: "Last night I asked Barry if we could see one of the 'girlie shows.' I was in the frame of mind to exercise my scientific observational tendencies. The night before, we had visited Patpong, where all the clubs are located. Barry took me into a club (at my request) where some Thai girls were dancing on an elaborate platform in the center of the floor. The girls were very pretty. The environment, at worst, was tacky . . . but it wasn't sleazy."

I had been in Bangkok countless times, but this was Mom's first time in Thailand. I had traveled to Thailand for work, because in the business I ran for J.P. Morgan, we were very active in the local financial markets of Thailand.

But I also traveled there for fun. I remember one of my first trips to Bangkok with three J.P. Morgan colleagues and also close friends (even today). One of them decided he was interested in one of the dancers in a bar in Patpong. Long story short, they ended up marrying and having a daughter with whom you both hung out on Phi Phi Island in Thailand on a return trip to Southeast Asia in 2010. Mom became friends with my colleague's Thai wife when we lived near each other in London in 1996. Mom was unique in her ability to connect with people from all walks of life and cultures and all levels of income, intelligence, and education. Mom did not have one pretentious bone in her body. She judged each individual she met by, as Martin Luther King Jr. said, "the contents of their character." She was indeed a special human being that the world needs a lot more of!

PRICE/KG
5.90
0.078
WEIGHT
TOTAL PRICE
0.46
Cold Storage
LYELL + DIANE HO
5 FALLING LEAF
IRVINE, CA 92
U.S.A.
XIENGTHONG TEMPLE LUANGPRABANG LAO P D R
Tel: 215724, 212263 Vientiane
SAMUI, THAILAND

4

The Magic of Burma and Laos with Mom (January 1995)

After a few days of some really good food in Bangkok, particularly at the restaurant Lemon Grass, we were ready to go to Burma, a country that I had never visited and really wanted to see. Mom wrote from Burma in her diary on January 15, 1995: "The people of Yangon, Myanmar (Burma) are completely inoffensive and generally friendly and lovely. Both the men and the women are lovely. Some say 'hello,' others avoid eye contact, but the women, children, and adolescent boys usually smile at you. In general, the people are much warmer than in India. We met a woman at the pagoda named May. She was Burmese, 18 years old, and very pretty. She acted as our guide and told us about the ancient holy relics. When we left she said, 'I have very good day today because I made a new friend.' Ditto on my part. This evening Barry and I returned to the pagoda. I think the moon was full. The pagoda was lit up and glowing gold. It was beautiful. We sat back and people-watched . . . the monks in their burgundy robes, men and women in sarongs, children and dogs. I could walk down any street in Yangon by myself in the evening . . . I might be slightly on guard, but I'm convinced nothing would happen to me. I like the people of Myanmar (Burma)."

From the length of Mom's journal entries on Burma (almost twenty pages) during the roughly two weeks we were there, it is clear that she loved the country, as did I. We had some very special experiences that I remember vividly to this day.

One of the best experiences in my travels with Mom was the day we stumbled upon a Buddhist monastery and were invited into the monks' dormitory room. Mom told the story better than I could in her diary entry from January 18, 1995: "Today was a glorious day. Barry and I rented bicycles and rode back to Marie-Mins Mandalay restaurant for breakfast. I had fresh muesli w/strawberries, papayas, bananas, pineapples, coconut, yogurt and a strawberry lassi. Afterwards we road through Mandalay towards Mandalay Hill where there was a pagoda at the top. Along the way, we stopped to drink some water and I was walking towards a garden and passed a group of Burmese soldiers. One asked, 'What country you from?' I said, 'United States.' They were a friendly lot . . . all smiling in a very unlecherous sort of way. I saw that one of them was wearing one of the Burmese army hats that I had been coveting. I said to the soldier, 'Hello.' They laughed, and one asked me, 'You like Myanmar?' I said, 'Yes, very much. The people are very kind and beautiful.' The solider said, 'Yes, Burmese very nice.' One of the soldiers said, 'You very pretty.' I said, 'Oh, no . . . people from Myanmar are very pretty . . . where I come from, I am very average.' [That was dear Mom being her typical humble self.] They laughed. I told the soldier with the hat, 'I like your hat.' He said, 'You keep it . . . a present.' I responded, 'Really? Thank you very much.' I took the new hat over to Barry and showed the trophy proudly to him.

"We continued on Mandalay Hill and parked our bikes. There was a school nearby. Children came at us everywhere shouting, 'Hello, hello' . . . boys and girls all smiling with their golden skin and dark eyes. Barry photographed many and actually went inside the school to take some photographs. Everyone here smiles wide beautiful smiles and many offer greetings!

"At the top of the hill we stopped and drank a 7-Up. The view of Mandalay was panoramic. As we were walking around a Buddhist monk came up to me and asked, 'What country do you come from?' After a nice discussion with the monk we walked to the (Mandalay) Buddhist University campus nearby. We stopped in front of a building that appeared to have dormitories. Some monks were walking by in various shades of red robes. One of them came up to us and asked, 'What do you want to know?' Barry asked, 'Can we come inside?' The monk responded, 'Yes, please come.' It was a clean room, green walls, a floor mat where the monk invited us to sit down. Barry did most of the questioning.

Jackie and Burmese monks, 1995

At one point, the monk told us that he was learning English and showed us some English tapes he had and a boombox and played the tape for us of a male and female Brit teaching English which was quite amusing to me and Barry. Sitting with these monks in this dorm room with Barry ranks among the most memorable moments of my life. For one thing, I love to be surrounded by men and in addition, I was surrounded by wonderful men . . . gentle men . . . men that oozed tranquility and sincerity and kindness through their pores . . . I could have sat there forever absorbing it all. We exchanged addresses and Barry took their photographs. The monks walked us out and bid us farewell. One said to me in English, 'May you always be happy in life' and smiled a warm, bright smile. We rode back towards the Royal Guest House. What a day!"

I have that day etched in my memory, mostly because I knew Mom was so content, on cloud nine. Later that day she gave me a big kiss and said, "Thank you for healing me." Those words gave me peace.

From Mandalay, Mom and I went to the ancient imperial capital of Burma, called Bagan. Mom wrote of Bagan: "I'm afraid my descriptions of Bagan will fall far short of relaying its beauty, but I'll make an attempt just for records' sake. First of all, Old Bagan is uncrowded, uncluttered with a backdrop of deep blue skies, fresh air, and warm sun. The climate that day was arid . . . rocky hills along the horizon. It is a desert, but you are aware of so much green and shade. Palm trees are clustered here and there, and there are pagodas everywhere. It becomes mesmerizing to look across the landscape and see these incredible structures . . . many in ruins, but so many in wonderful condition. They appear very naturally in their setting, most are constructed out of sandstone . . . some red and others white with golden tops. The walls inside of many of the ones we visited had remnants of Buddhist paintings, lotus pattern ceilings. The statues of Buddhas and disciples varied. I saw two reclining Buddhas, both incredibly large. There were four standing Buddhas all in gold leaf . . . magnificent. We climbed the stairs from one pagoda and from the top you could see all of Bagan in its splendor . . . over 5,000 of these structures amidst the beauty of Myanmar. When you see Bagan, it is incredibly awesome and you can leave it up to your imagination to envision it as it was in its prime, from the eleventh to thirteenth century . . . and it is easy to envision it and absorb its magnificence because it has remained quite untainted by tourism. . . . . you don't see hotels, restaurants and shops everywhere. Our guide said, 'I would never want to live anywhere else in the world.' But he had never been outside of Myanmar . . . but Barry, who has traveled the world over, said he had never seen any place more awe-inspiring . . . you can easily believe it. The beauty of Bagan is carried out through her people as well. They are appealing, and they exemplify Buddhism at its best."

That evening we ate dinner in Old Bagan at the nondescript River View restaurant. We had a nice conversation with the manager. She talked about her dreams of opening up her own restaurant. Mom wrote: "Her demeanor was very sweet, very warm. She sat with us and talked through dinner. Barry kept asking questions regarding the cost of setting up a guesthouse, which was her

Ancient Bagan, Burma, 1995

dream. In the end, he was ready to loan her the money to build her own guesthouse in Bagan. It was utterly touching and also a realization for me that Barry probably had a good bit of money. I found that unsettling . . . I don't know why."

In a world so driven by materiality, it was refreshing and a joy to be around Mom, who was not driven in the least by money. On the drive back to Mandalay from Bagan we stopped at a small roadside town, so Mom could use the bathroom. I followed Mom toward the back where the bathrooms were and, as she described: "There were some people pounding rocks into pebbles. I could not see their faces as they were shielded by the palm branches. When I finished in the outhouse, I opened the door, and Barry was standing next to an old woman by the rock pile. Barry asked me, 'Did you see the girl there pounding rocks?' I said 'no.' He said, 'She is very beautiful, look at her.' So I walked over and peered around the palm branch where I could see a small female figure sitting. She stopped pounding the rocks and looked over at me timidly. Barry

Burmese girl and Jackie, 1995

was right, this girl was absolutely beautiful. Her face was classic . . . oval, with high cheekbones upon which the flesh formed perfect small mounds. She had noticeable lips, not too full, but beautiful. Her eyes were dream-eyes . . . dark brows and lashes, the pupils light brown. Her hair was tied back in one long braid that went past her hips. She was very slight, small wrists, slender neck and she looked at me not sure of what my intentions were. I smiled at her and walked back to Barry and said, 'You're right, she's stunning!' Barry said, 'I cannot believe this beautiful little girl is sitting back here pounding rocks.' We found out that she was a girl from the village, unmarried and working pounding rocks with her father."

After some back-and-forth with the owner of the shop, we were given permission to take her picture. Mom continued: "Barry took his camera out, and she consented to her being photographed. She was truly lovely!" Afterwards,

Jackie with Burmese boys, 1995

Barry handed me some money to give her. I walked over and handed her the money and said, 'Kyay zoo tin laa' [presumably, This is for you]. She smiled demurely accepting the money. Barry said, 'It kills me to see her sitting there like that all day.'" Mom was curious why I took such an interest in this young girl. She wrote: "I asked Barry if his attraction towards this girl was sexual, and he said 'No, not at all . . . it is admiration, like a nice painting.'"

I loved Mom's last entry in Burma while we were at the train station in Mandalay to take the train back to Yangon, the capital, on our way out of Burma: "While Barry was reading the newspaper, 2 boys came over to sell us some water. We declined, and they casually sat down in front of us and looked at us and talked between them. Pretty soon about 4 other boys joined the first two. I noticed that one of them had a tattoo on his forearm and I bent down to look at it. He showed me two more on his arms. Then he showed me several other ones on the arms of the other boys sitting down. I showed them my tattoo and they were greatly amused . . . as were the soldiers. A man sitting on a bench said, 'Sunflower.' I said, 'Yes.' My tattoo had been useful on several occasions as an icebreaker . . . I'm kind of glad I have it!"

Unbelievably, Mom used to tell me that she thought she was shy. Our usual team approach to meeting new people, whether locals or other tourists, was that I would start off some kind of conversation. Before long, Mom would take over and be engrossed in discussing whatever came to her mind. In the end, people would fall in love with Mom.

On January 27, 1995, we were in Koh Samui in Thailand, which Mom described this way: "It was absolutely beautiful, this island and the guesthouse we stayed at was perfect, a bungalow right on the beach . . . beautiful aquamarine water, white sand beach, coconut palms, sunshine, and balmy air. At night, we ate scrumptious Thai food at a nearby restaurant after drinking beers and playing backgammon at the bar next door. We also rented mopeds and cruised around the island. This was our routine for four days."

I remember Mom getting in a bit of a nasty moped accident. She scraped her knee pretty badly, but somehow, she did not write about that in her journal. I also remember watching the San Francisco 49ers crush the San Diego Chargers in the Super Bowl from a bar by the beach.

Mom and I got into our only big argument of our entire six months traveling together while we were in Koh Samui. In her diary she wrote a letter to her friend Karen: "Dearest Karen, you are so far away from me and I long to be sitting next to you, engaging in conversation, hearing about your life, asking you questions, telling you of my adventures. All yesterday, I thought I was picking up a bit of tension and some bad vibes from Barry. Sometimes, I honestly don't know what men want and I think I have come to the realization that the male species can be the most difficult to deal with at times." Mom did end the entry with a bit of humor, saying, "Men, sometimes you can't live with them, but you can't shoot them." As usual, by the next day whatever our argument was about was forgotten.

In a postcard to Grandma and Grandpa on January 29, 1995, Mom wrote: "Dear Mom & Dad, I'll be brief on this card, because I just spoke with you but I

SAMUI, THAILAND

1/29/95

Suchilla art Studio, Bkk, TEL: (02)7516068

Dear Mom + Dad - I'll be brief on this card, because I just spoke with you, but I had to send you a post card of this place... it's absolute paradise! Brian + Jen should come here on their honeymoon. Anyways, I'm thoroughly enjoying myself here and hope all is well with you. I also have a favor to ask mom... I figured since she might have some extra time on her hands she could help me out in investigating locations of Nursing Schools + Physician assistance programs in Southern California + Bay Area... also, if you could have them send applications. UCI or Irvine Valley college might have listings of programs. If its difficult, don't worry about it, I'll do it when I get back, but it would save me time + I can get started on the process quickly when I get back. Thanks!

Love, [illegible]

Chaweng Beach, Samui Island

Lyell + Diane Holmes
5 Falling Leaf
Irvine, CA
92715
U.S.A.

A postcard from Koh Samui, Thailand, 1995

had to send you a postcard of this place . . . it's absolute paradise! Love, Jackie." After four days we were back in Bangkok ready for the next leg of our travels. At that point, we were still shooting for Vietnam. Mom writes: "That evening we ate, again, at Lemon Grass Restaurant in Bangkok . . . DIVINE. Before leaving for Koh Samui, Barry told me that he had a surprise for me and would tell me in a week what it was. So, for the entire week he entertained himself by giving me misleading hints about what the surprise was. He is such an imp! I was resolved that the surprise was that there was no surprise or that he was shipping me back home, having had enough of me. Our original plan was to spend a few days in Vietnam and, while waiting for our visas for China, touring the country. It turned out that due to Chinese New Year the Chinese Embassy in Vietnam would be closed for another week. Barry didn't tell me this of course and re-routed us to Laos, a country I had mentioned that I would love to see. I was very happy with this surprise, but would have liked to have toured Vietnam. Mainly, I was relieved that I would still be travelling with Barry, as I am very fond of him."

By this time, Mom and I had been traveling for about six weeks and had been together over one month. We had seen and experienced so many amazing things in such a short time, had fallen in love, had so many good times together and even a big argument. I was having the time of my life and really did not feel like that trip was a vacation. It felt way more permanent, like the beginning of a lifetime of adventure with my soul mate.

We arrived in Vientiane, the capital of Laos, on January 31, 1995. Mom wrote: "So here we are in Vientiane, the capital of Laos and even less-capital-city-seeming than Yangon. It is very provincial, less crowded and much smaller. It's a strange little town, lacking in a culture it can call its own. The teenagers all wear western clothes unlike the teenagers of Myanmar . . . and trendy clothes at that, i.e., Dock Martens shoes, loose-fitting Levi's, etc."

From there we went to the ancient provincial capital of Laos, Luang Prabang. Along with Bagan, in Burma, Luang Prabang was one of Mom's favorite places: "About 200km north of Vientiane along the Mekong and Nam Kuhn Rivers is the city of Luang Prabang. The city gets its name from a Sinhalese Buddha image from Angkor Wat; it was a gift from the Khmer monarchy to

Jackie, Luang Prabang, Laos, 1995

King Fa Ngum, who ruled the Lao Kingdom of Lan Xang in the mid-fourteenth century. The last ruling monarch, Sisavang Vatthana, was removed by the Pathet Lao in 1975. The town is cool and lush . . . coconut palms, teak, bamboo trees, shrubs, grass. Along the banks of the two rivers are garden plots with vegetables of all sorts growing in rows and patches. There are several Buddhist wats here and with them Buddhist monks adorned in the orange robes and shaven heads. When you roam the streets here (and there are only a few of them to roam) you see children everywhere . . . beautiful children . . . happy and healthy and very friendly! Barry and I are staying at the Villa de la Princess, and it is a dream. The hotel used to be the home of the princess. Later in the morning, Barry and I took a walk through the town and walked upstairs, lined with dragons to the top of a temple where a golden Buddha was enshrined at the top of a hill. I left $5 and my favorite pen . . . for good Karma toward getting into China."

That night, Mom and I discussed the possibility that she, without a visa to enter China, would not get in at the Laos-China border but that I would and whether she was seriously willing to travel back to Vientiane to get a visa and fly to meet me in Kunming, China. While I did worry about Mom traveling by herself, despite Laos being a very safe country, I knew that I selfishly wanted to travel overland to China and not fly. I had always felt incredible excitement at remote border crossings like Argentina-Bolivia or El Salvador-Guatemala, and this was one of the more remote border outposts. In those days, there was no internet and very little information on this border, so we really had no good idea whether, even with a visa to China, we could get through. We were going to travel north in Laos, to the border, on the fly, and would give it a shot. I was very grateful to Mom for being willing to let me experience this adventure.

Mom really loved Luang Prabang, writing in her postcard to Grandma and Grandpa, on February 3, 1995: "Dear Mom & Dad, a note to let you know that I received the package, including the money (thank you very much), in Bangkok. As you can see from the postcard, we are in Laos instead of Vietnam. We decided to come here because the Vietnamese Embassy was closed in Bangkok due to the Chinese New Year's . . . and the Laos Embassy wasn't. So here we are! Vientiane is the smallest capital city I have ever seen. We spent about a day and a half here and then flew north to Luang Prabang. It's absolutely beautiful here . . . we're sitting in this little open-air restaurant overlooking the Mekong River. It's very lush with coconut palms, etc., and very laid back. There are many Buddhist temples here like the one on the front of this card, many monks, and many beautiful children. Tomorrow we are taking a boat up the Mekong, then driving to the Chinese border where we will try to cross into China's Yunnan Province. I'll write more later. Love, Jackie."

During our travels through these very Buddhist towns in Burma and Laos, it hit me that Mom, in her heart, was very Buddhist-like, and she exemplified the best qualities of this great religion: compassion, loving-kindness, and empathic joy.

Mom continued about our trip from Luang Prabang up the Mekong River by boat toward the Laos-China border: "On the morning of February 4, 1995, we took a speedboat up the Mekong. The trip up the Mekong, despite the noise from the boat engine and wind chill, was magnificent. The sun over the lush green hills, white sand banks with buffalo sun-bathing. Fishing villages along the way, natural rock sculptures, fishing boats, people, Lao villagers on the

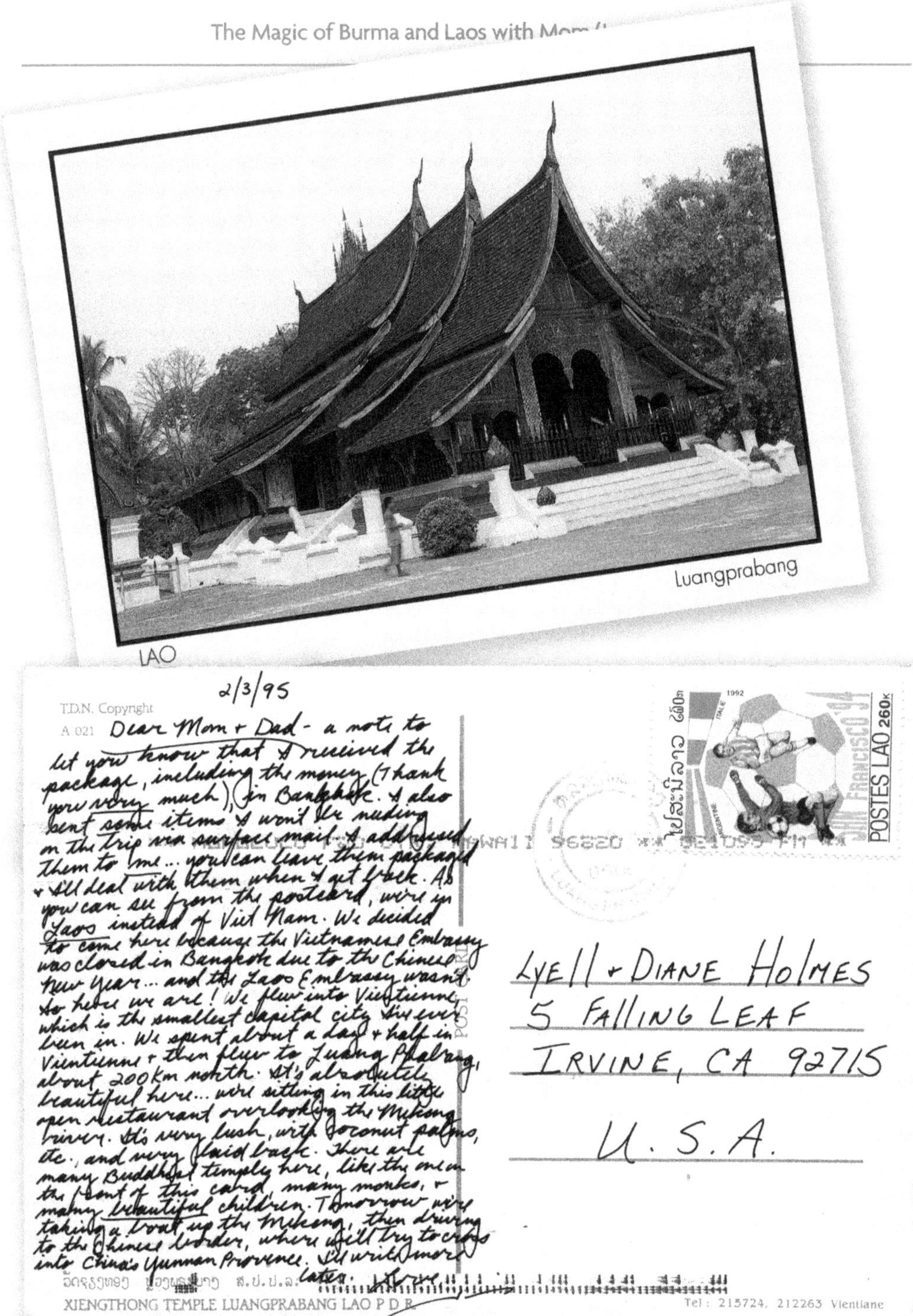

2/3/95

Dear Mom + Dad - a note to let you know that I received the package, including the money (Thank you very much), in Bangkok. I also sent some items I won't be needing on the trip via surface mail. I addressed them to me... you can leave them packaged + I'll deal with them when I get back. As you can see from the postcard, we're in Laos instead of Viet Nam. We decided to come here because the Vietnamese Embassy was closed in Bangkok due to the Chinese New Year... and the Laos Embassy wasn't. So here we are! We flew into Vientienne, which is the smallest capital city I've ever been in. We spent about a day + half in Vientienne + then flew to Luang Phabang, about 200km north. It's absolutely beautiful here... we're sitting in this little open restaurant overlooking the Mekong river. It's very lush, with coconut palms, etc., and very laid back. There are many Buddhist temples here, like the one on the front of this card, many monks, + many beautiful children. Tomorrow we're taking a boat up the Mekong, then driving to the Chinese border, where we'll try to cross into China's Yunnan Province. I'll write more later. Love,

Lyell + Diane Holmes
5 Falling Leaf
Irvine, CA 92715
U.S.A.

A postcard from Luang Prabang, Laos, 1995

Monks in Luang Prabang, Laos, 1995

banks checking nets, bathing, children playing and, of course, this vast body of water on which we were speeding up while it flowed south. The sunset over the Mekong was special! We spent the night at some non-descript, less-than-clean hotel. Barry and I had decided we'd try to enter China through Boten, a northern Lao city that borders China . . . but that if I did not get in and he did, I would travel back to Vientiane and fly to Kunming, China, to meet him. My gut feeling was that Barry would get in and I wouldn't . . . the good karma tokens could be put towards my return trip to Vientiane in case I didn't get in."

A sunset on the Mekong, Laos, 1995

As I was mentally getting ready to approach the border the next day, and then hopefully enter China, I was torn between some worry for Mom not getting in, traveling back to Vientiane, and flying to Kunming by herself and my own thrill, but also selfishness, in being determined to travel overland instead of flying with Mom. I don't like to make excuses for myself, but I had led a very independent life for the previous sixteen years and lived on my own, with the exception of three months, for the previous ten years. I had not yet learned the art of compromise for someone I cared about. Nonetheless, not once did Mom say anything about not wanting me to go through with my plans if she did not get in at the border.

In a way, my admiration grew markedly for Mom's willingness to go back on her own to Vientiane. She showed her independence, determination, and sense of adventure. Mom wrote: "Barry arranged a ride for us the next morning with some very spacey, shady characters, in the back of a truck, up to the Chinese border. Barry surmised that they were involved in some kind of car-smuggling ring. Unfortunately, I did not make it across the border . . . Barry gave me all his cash, credit card and a look of reservation/concern and I got in the back of a truck for my return journey to Vientiane. I rode with 4 other Lao women and 2 Lao men."

In hindsight, it may have been best that Mom did not travel with me overland from the Laos-China border to Kunming. My journey proved to be a very rough, dirty three-day trip with long overcrowded bus rides. When I met up with Mom a few days later, she was rightly proud of her own little solo journey.

Mom continued about her return trip: "The women were like women in most parts of the world . . . I would imagine . . . very much into conversing, comforting towards me in a way that was perhaps negligible to most men. Every time they brought out food, they would offer it to me, encouraging me to take it. The language they spoke, which may have been Lao, or some tribal language, was amazing to listen to . . . very sing-song. At times their voices would rise to a very high pitch."

I don't think I will ever forget the vision of Mom sitting in the back of that Toyota pickup truck with a number of other Laotian women in beautiful traditional dress.

The next day, Mom arrived in Vientiane to both secure her visa for China and catch a flight to Kunming. In the meantime, I was on a harrowing journey from the Laos-China border through Yunnan Province on my way to Kunming, Yunnan's capital city.

Yunnan is one of China's most interesting and certainly most diverse provinces. It is home to twenty-five different ethnic groups whereas in all of China's twenty-three provinces there are fifty-six ethnic groups. My trip to Kunming took roughly two-and-a-half days on two different, long bus rides, with one

Laotian women at the border between Laos and China, 1995

night's stay in between at a very shady, disgusting hotel. I was the only foreigner, the buses were old, it was freezing cold, and everyone seemed to love spitting on the floor. At one point, there was so much spit on the floor under the seat in front of me that when the bus went uphill, there was a nice little stream of spit making its way right toward me. Those were not the days of simply plugging in your earbuds into your iPhone and escaping. For me, the only foreigner, the sounds and smells that came from that overcrowded bus made for a less than comfortable journey. Nonetheless, it was quite thrilling and interesting, though I was greatly missing Mom. We had been inseparable for a long time before Mom headed back to Vientiane. We didn't have email and cell phones then, so it was impossible to keep in touch with her. We simply made concrete plans

LAOS TO CHINA

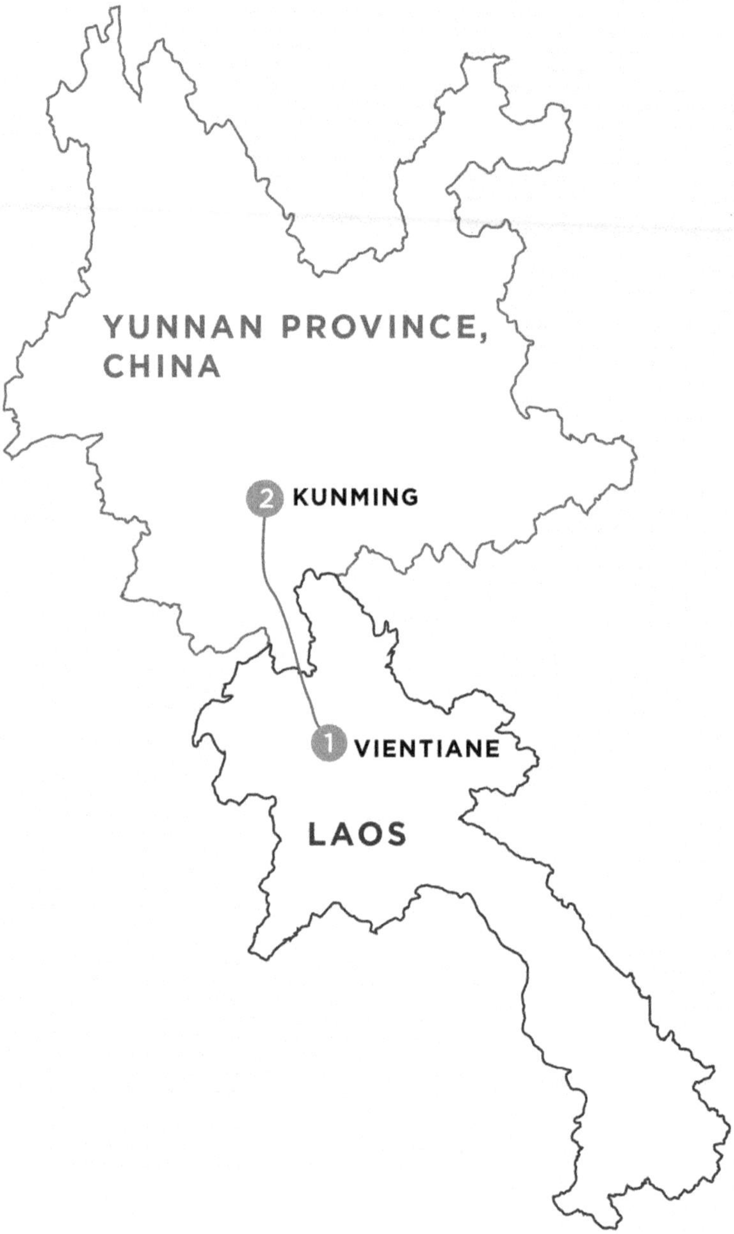

to meet at the Kunming Hotel in Kunming and guessed the first likely day we would be there. We also agreed to meet there every day at a specific time for the following three or four days, just in case either of us got delayed.

In the meantime, Mom was in Vientiane and on her way to the Chinese Embassy to get her visa. She wrote: "I asked someone where the Chinese embassy was. A man said to me, 'This policeman will take you there,' which he did. I thanked the policeman. I rang the buzzer, but no one answered. Unfortunately, it was already closed for the day . . . I'll be there at 8:00am tomorrow morning . . . I hope to Buddha that someone there speaks English . . . but just in case, I'll learn a bit of Chinese this evening. I arrived at the embassy at 8:55am . . . a woman came and unlocked the gate. 'Bonjour,' she said. Bonjour, vous parlez Anglais?' I asked. 'Non, non . . . je parle Francias,' she said smiling. I was skeptical of being able to communicate the necessity of me getting my visa that day in French. She led me into an office. She was obviously the only one working there. I said, 'Je voudrais un visa pour Chine . . . mais . . . aujourdhui . . . parce que je depart pour Chine demain . . . c'est possible?' Not only did she understand but her response was pleasing . . . 'Oui . . . mais tu attendre pour treinte minute, si-tu-plait . . . ,' she said, or something like that. I couldn't believe I was actually going to have a visa for China in thirty minutes. I received the visa just a bit later and thanked her very much in English, French and Chinese. Next stop: Lao Aviation. The woman said that yes, there was a flight to Kunming tomorrow, and yes, I could pay by credit card. . . . However, I had never practiced forging Barry's signature, so I just went ahead and signed my name. This didn't work so I ended up depleting Barry's cash. I did end up, however, getting a refund for our unused tickets from Luang Prabang to Vientiane. At least that adds a little bit to the kitty. I'm trying to return as much as possible to Mr. Hoffner . . . who I'm looking forward to meeting in China. But while I miss him, I am also glad to have had the time to brush up on my traveling skills these past days. As I was leaving, I met some children who were playing on the sidewalk . . . three of them said to me, 'Hello madame. Where you come from?' I said, 'Hello . . . from the United States' . . . they asked, 'What's your name?' . . . 'Jackie, what are yours?' They all separately told me their names but having no reference for Lao names, I can't recall them. They were sweet children with smiles."

At that moment, I was probably back on the bus for the second leg of that journey to Kunming after a night's stay in a really sleazy hotel. It seemed to be a hotel where the ladies of the town worked, and I finally disconnected the telephone in my room after a few calls from some working ladies. Clearly, the management of this disgusting hotel was involved in this business.

On February 9, 1995, Mom reached our meeting point at the Kunming Hotel in Kunming, China, not knowing whether or not I had already arrived. Here is dear Mom's entry from that special day: "I'm sitting in the lobby of the Kunming Hotel, waiting for Barry . . . and when I see him, I know I am going to be *thrilled* . . . right now, I'm feeling a bit anxious, because there's a chance I've arrived in Kunming before him and god only knows what I'm going to do here . . . where I'll stay, etc. I'm sure I'll get by . . . somehow. This morning in Vientiane, before my flight, I bought some great-looking French bread, smoked salmon and an onion to go with yesterday's purchases of garlic, basil, tomatoes, and camembert cheese. I also bought a bottle of Bordeaux wine at the duty-free shop to go with . . . now I need a wine opener. I hope Barry will be as thrilled about my purchases as I am . . . I thought we could have a reunion feast."

It's funny, but Mom and I had spent practically every waking hour together for more than two months such that three days apart seemed quite long indeed. Before Mom left on her flight from Vientiane to Kunming, she did manage to call everyone back home. "I found a telephone, telegraph place advertising international calls so I went in and placed a call to Julie's and had her call me back with Julie, Mom, Bradley and Roger. I miss them all!" I loved how Mom always spoke so lovingly about all of her family and was particularly pleased to have a nephew, Bradley. I really had never met a woman so centered around family. Having grown up very much on my own after the divorce of my parents (Baba Toba and Papa Dave) when I was around the age of seven, I was always ready for a new adventure, never thinking twice about missing family. I knew that Mom was having the time of her life on our trip but also that she missed home.

a paneer roll, +
content.
stare at us... not in an
was wearing an outfit that
covered, &
background
and pink
the men in

5

Living as Students in a Dormitory in China (February 1995)

Here is Mom's first reaction to people in China after being there just a few hours: "From what I can tell of China so far, the people definitely have an attitude. . . . I'm sure this might be a bit premature of an opinion, but I bet the rest of my time here proves it right [Mom's first insight was right]. When I arrived in the hotel lobby, I walked to the desk of the assistant manager and asked her if there was a place I could leave my bags because I was meeting a friend there in a couple of hours. She cut me off and said, 'What room number you stay in?' I said, 'I'm not staying here, I'm meet—' . . . She cut me off again, 'If you don't have a room here, I can't help you,' and she abruptly walked away. So, I found a sofa, parked my bags next to it and sat down . . . which is where I am now . . . waiting for Mr. Hoffner. If he doesn't show, I can't complain . . . everything has gone very smoothly thus far, and I made it to Kunming. I think my offering to Buddha has paid off."

Mom and I did meet up that day, exactly as we had hoped, and spent the night in a hotel. The next day we enrolled at Yunnan University, in the Chinese program for foreigners, and rented a very basic room together for $10 a day. We had one hour of hot water in the morning and evening, each at a specific time. I look back at that period so incredibly fondly. Mom and I had been traveling almost nonstop for about ten weeks, and this gave us the chance to be in one place for a good bit of time with other students, also learning Mandarin, from all around the world. Mom described Kunming this way: "As for Kunming, it is a very livable city. Also known as Spring City, it seems to be in a suspended state of the season and thus appropriately named. The people of Kunming are not warm . . . rather chilly and aggressive and don't hesitate making you feel foolish at times, generally speaking. For the most part, they do not go out of their way to understand you and often act annoyed at your inability to communicate in their language. But I do find the peoples' attitude refreshing and motivating. It is sink or swim as far as communication goes, and when people are abrasive to you it cultivates an abrasive/aggressive attitude in you as well and hence is energizing. There are exceptions."

I had already been studying Mandarin while living in Singapore for the previous year and a half. I could read and write roughly a thousand characters and could carry on a reasonable conversation. But Mom had started from scratch. I admired how willing she was to put herself out of her comfort zone and try to learn some Mandarin. Mom truly had an inherent spirit of adventure that matched my own.

Mom and I also did some wonderful trips throughout Yunnan Province, mostly traveling via overnight bus ride. Specifically, we went to the towns of Dali and Lijiang and also took a memorable multiday trek in an area called Tiger Leaping Gorge. We always seemed to meet cool people and often enjoyed their company traveling with us. People always gravitated to Mom's sun-filled personality. Mom always loved to describe the people we met.

Dali was one of the most popular tourist destinations in Yunnan Province, known for its natural scenery, history, and cultural heritage. Dali, formerly known as Xiaguan, was an important trading center for people traveling from Tibet, Burma, Laos, and the Chinese mountain districts. Mom described the city: "Dali was a watering hole for Westerners, but a welcomed one, unless you are trying to improve your Mandarin." We hung out in Dali about a week and got to know a number of people there. Mom mentioned some of the people we hung out with and the nicknames we gave them: "Eric, 'the student,' a thirty-three-year-old graduate of Chinese History, and Dick, 'the Captain,' and his wife, 'the Spacer,' who works for UNESCO, and Vernon," 'the professor,' studying local 'games' in small Chinese towns and 'the Lifer.' I don't know his real name, but he came to Dali months ago and has no plans to leave anytime soon. Barry is 'the banker.' I don't know what I am, but Eric and Barry will come

SIDE TRIPS IN YUNNAN PROVINCE, CHINA

up with something. Among other people we met in Dali are Iris and Eran, a couple from Israel whom I like very much. We have been traveling a bit with them and they are ideal travel partners. Iris is gifted in the art of persuasion and Eric and Barry have nicknamed her the 'negociator.' We have also made some local friends . . . Jack the owner and operator of Café de Jack. He speaks perfect street English with an American accent. His restaurant/bar has the best food and ambience in town. Mei Di is a *beautiful* woman that has a shop where she gives *wonderful* facials for 25 yuan for 1 hour. She is thirty years old but looks no older than twenty-three."

Mom described our trip to Lijiang from Dali: "We left Dali yesterday and took a five-hour bus ride to Lijiang. The landscape was beautiful, and the morning sunlight amplified the beauty. Mountains in the background, patches of green, yellow and red, villages with beautiful Chinese architecture . . . and the people. We stopped at a market. It was a visual delight with baskets of vegetables, grains, fish, cloth, paper, wares and the Bai people all in traditional dress . . . blue and black with elaborate, bright head pieces, pink, blue, orange, red, and black. The children were the best!" The Bai people live mostly in Yunnan Province and constitute one of the 56 ethnic groups officially recognized by the Chinese government. They are known for their colorful dress and handicraft work. Many still speak their original Bai language and live communally.

Lijiang is a UNESCO World Heritage city that has a history dating back over a thousand years. It became an important artisanal center for carvings, dancing, and music by the indigenous Nakhi people. Mom wrote: "It is a city that fortunately has maintained its old city, and that is where Barry and I took a walk yesterday through narrow, cobbled streets with wonderful Chinese-style dwellings on each side, with tiled roofs, large wooden doorways and Nakhi people walk about . . . the old women in their blue-black dresses. . . . It's cold here but I am getting used to it." The Nahki people also are one of the 56 recognized ethnic groups in China. They have their own language, writing, and dress and are well known for their beautiful music. Sadly, a year after we were there, in February 1996, a large 6.6 earthquake struck the heart of Lijiang, killing more than three hundred people and destroying more than two hundred thousand structures.

Rooftops of Lijiang, China, 1995

Mom and I also traveled to the Tiger Leaping Gorge. She wrote: "We set out for the gorge at about 10am . . . about three hours later we finally found the path to begin our trek. We crossed the Yangtze River and climbed uphill for about 45 minutes. For me, at times, it was tortuous because of my vertigo [which dear Mom failed to mention to me until a good way through the trek] . . . we had to cross about 4 landslide areas where the footpath was very narrow and unstable . . . after that we saw very little of the Yangtze River but the inland hills were beautiful and mile-high mountains on the other side of the river were visible. At one point we passed two men, probably Nakhi, with their horse mule. I made Barry take a picture of these weathered, smiling men and their beast in the isolated hills and mountains with blue sky and white suspended clouds. When we finally caught site of the Yangtze, it was beautiful. We stayed the first night at Sean's Place. It was rustic but a goldmine, particularly after our unexpectedly long day. It was only 5 kwai (a few $$) for a bed

Barry and Jackie, Tiger Leaping Gorge, Yangtse River, China, 1995

and free hot shower, reasonably priced and excellent food with yak cheese and Chinese-style burritos. There were about 7 other Western trekkers . . . we all sat that night together around the one table next to the kitchen and talked, ate and kept warm."

We finished our trek a few days later, and after waiting for a public bus that never came, we decided to try our luck at hitchhiking back to Lijiang. Mom wrote: "Within an hour, one of the plush tour buses carrying Taiwanese tourists pulled over and picked us up. It was going to Lijiang. Not only did it take us, it also dropped us off right in front of our guesthouse *AND* it didn't charge us anything. *Karma!!!* Praise be God! Barry and I have been fortunate in finding two such awesome traveling companions as Iris and Eran, an Israeli couple (Iris' birthday is Oct 21st!!)." Mom's entry that day had a cute ending: "*Digression:* On the first day of the trek, we stopped at a very small village for lunch . . . the Shop Pepsi (not Pepsi Shop). We sat on the front porch of the house where a Nakhi family lived and served us. There was a baby goat that hung out with us through our meal and ate whatever we gave it . . . and the chickens came begging. *End of Digression.*"

Again, I admired Mom's adventurous spirit, particularly given that she was fearful of heights, something I only learned during the middle of the trek. I recently came across this description of the Tiger Leaping Gorge Trek in a guidebook: "It seems inadequate to call this a hike. After spending thirty hours on the trail, it might qualify as borderline mountaineering!" At a maximum depth of roughly 12,000 feet from the river to the top of the surrounding peak, Tiger Leaping Gorge is one of the deepest and most spectacular river canyons in the world."

Mom and I had both enrolled in the Mandarin program for foreigners at Yunnan University, in Kunming, Yunnan Province. We got a room together in the dormitories for foreigners. Something like twenty-five or so other students were also there, studying Mandarin at different levels. By then I was in an intermediate class, and Mom was just starting out. Something like half of the foreigners were from Italy, and we quickly became very close with many of them. I think Mom developed her love for all things Italian through our friendships with the Italians who were studying Mandarin and living in the dorms with us.

Mom described the Italians we met in Kunming:

Matteo "hubba, hubba"
(Benjamin, you actually met Matteo twice. The first time was in February 1998, when you were only five months old. You, Mom, and I took a trip to Venice to visit Matteo and Alessia. You met him again in Venice after you graduated from Brandeis in 2012 and I took you on a three-week trip to Italy.)
Alessia "Matteo's girlfriend"
Valentina "a sweet, warm girl. Very serious about learning Chinese"
Georgia "very nice, very pretty"
Lara "Knows how to have fun"
"I love the Italians."

As I look back now, our time in Kunming was one of the most interesting, simple, peaceful, and wonderful periods of my life. Nothing to worry about, as

I was not working, and simple in the sense that we had no TV, cellphones, or internet. Just Mom and me together in our dorm, surrounded by a number of newly made friends from all over the world, studying Mandarin and learning about China firsthand. Even today, I long for that kind of adventurous, authentic, and simple existence, particularly doing it with a lifelong partner. I think about the income and career opportunity I gave up for that sabbatical, and it pales in comparison to these experiences with Mom and the rich memories that will stay with me the rest of my life. Motto of the Day: "When in doubt, go with your heart AND opt for adventure!"

Kunming, in those days, was one of China's nicer large cities, still with a lot of traditional architecture and little pollution. Mom described the area where we lived: "The city is pleasant, visually, with trees lining many of the streets, old architecture still in existence and a well-designed plan in general. The campus of Yunnan University is also appealing to walk through, as is the area around Green Lake. There is no noticeable smog in Kunming, but there is wind which carries, through the streets, dust and debris and dry air that impales your nostrils and eyes and dehydrates your skin." On the face of it, as Mom and I were ten and fifteen years removed from college life, it should have been strange to be living in a dormitory, studying at a university with students half our age, but it was not.

I remember Mom and me eating at a little Chinese rice stand in Kunming. The family that owned the place was so nice, but the first meal we had there was awful. That was partly my fault, as generally we were trying to be vegetarian in China due to the poor quality of meat. I asked if they had chicken and they responded yes. So, I ordered chicken. They basically lowered a whole, gutted chicken into a deep fryer, put it on a plate, and served it to us. We barely ate any of it. However, the owner's daughter, Louisa, who was learning English, quickly became our close friend. Louisa's English was very proper, and she often used words in a strange way. After spending a day with us around Kunming, when we said goodbye, she said, "Barry and Jackie, I am feeling so beautiful" as a way of colloquially telling us that she felt great after meeting us. Mom and I would often stop at their rice stand to say hi and chat. The family wanted to open a café that catered more to the growing number of foreigners in Kunming, so

Jackie in Mandarin class, Yunnan University, Kunming, China, 1995

Mom spent many afternoons teaching them how to cook a number of American dishes: pasta, pizza, sandwiches, omelets, and so on.

Mom's entry about meeting Louisa and her family was: "We have walked miles in this city and discovered streets, shops, and restaurants that I favor. One such restaurant Barry actually stumbled upon serendipitously . . . there is a young woman there named Zher Juin, also known as Louisa, who speaks very good English. She is warm and sunny and welcoming. Her family owns the restaurant and Barry and I have had many outstanding dishes there."

Mom wrote on March 15, 1995: "It's been three weeks since last I made notes on my journey through Asia . . . probably because my journey has come to a halt here in Kunming where Barry and I have settled in at Yunnan University 'Center of Chinese for Foreign Students.' We are in the middle of the third week of classes and to be honest, I'm quite disappointed and frustrated with my progress in learning a bit of the Chinese language. My teachers speak way too much English in class, and several of the students should be taking a

Barry's thirty-fifth birthday dinner, Kunming, China, 1995

Chinese history course (taught in English) instead of trying to learn to speak Chinese."

My birthday was coming up, April 16, and Mom was determined to throw me a surprise birthday party. She enlisted the Italians to make a big pasta birthday dinner. The Italians were adamant about needing olive oil, which was impossible to find in Kunming at that time. Finally, Mom went to a cosmetic shop that carried olive oil, which well-off Chinese women put on their skin as a moisturizer. My friend Mei came from Singapore to visit us. She recalled: "I remember Jackie was stressing over getting olive oil, a key ingredient, and she didn't want to use just any regular oil. Back then, it was not something you can find in a Chinese supermarket. But she was a resourceful one. She found olive oil sold in cosmetic counters that Chinese ladies use as a moisturizer, make-up remover, or even for the hair. Because I am Chinese and read Mandarin, I found myself helping Jackie by scouring over bottles of olive oil to check for the ones that are all natural with no addition of scented ingredients. The food turned out well!" We had the dinner at Luisa's parents' new restaurant focused on Western dishes, many of which Mom was responsible for teaching them how to cook. Grandma and Grandpa also sent us a nice "care package" with my favorite licorice for my birthday and *The Economist* magazine as well, despite the fact that I had never met or spoken with them. Grandpa and Grandma are so thoughtful!

Another funny story was Mom practicing her Mandarin on a taxi driver. Mom always used to talk about dogs (gou), particularly about little Gryphen. She even gave Gryphen her own Chinese name complete with Chinese characters, which I don't remember. One day we got in a taxi and I asked the driver to take us to a good restaurant for dinner. He asked what kind of food we liked. Mom was not following the conversation in Mandarin but just then decided to make small talk with the driver. She piped in and said, "Wo xi huan gou" (I like dog). The taxi driver thought that we wanted to go to a restaurant where they serve dog. I had to explain that Mom meant that she liked dogs as pets, not to eat. After a while, Mom, understandably, had enough of China. She was healed from her earlier troubles and wanted to return home. I remember a bad experience Mom had buying some fruit from a fruit peddler one day. I could tell she was losing patience with the rough attitude of many of the people one has to interact with on the street. In her diary, she described the encounter: "'Before you told me that these oranges cost 3 kwai, so I gave you 10. Now, you tell me that they are 9 kwai, so now I don't want them.' The peasant was livid and shouting at me and all the men around were amused. I walked away feeling good that I was able to defend myself and in Mandarin."

She wrote on April 21, 1995: "At the end of March, I reached a saturation point for China . . . my tolerance level had peaked and I was ready to return home to the United States. I reached this on one of my worst days in Kunming when I was passing a man right when he decided to spit . . . the same spit hit the side of my face. Then I was walking down the street and tripped and fell on my face and no one stopped to help me . . . I didn't expect them to . . . thus, at the end March I had had enough . . . of people spitting on buses, in restaurants, of shop attendants scowling at me and my poor communications skills, of dirt and wind. On April 1, I told Barry that I would be leaving in a few weeks. On

April 2, I woke up and my resentment I had built up against China and her people was gone, and a feeling of acceptance and tolerance had replaced it. I don't know what made me convert, but I had changed my attitude. I have learned from Barry. He approaches a person's abrasive attitude as a challenge . . . and works the people over until he gets them to smile or at least lighten up a bit . . . so I adopted this approach. I was trying to buy a pair of shoes and as usual the woman was rude, scowled at me, as I expected. But instead of leaving the store pissed, I decided to chat her up. . . . So I asked her if she liked the shoes I was trying on. She said yes. Then I told her my husband had told me I should buy some new shoes. She smiled!"

During Mom's last week in Kunming we met up with one of our dorm friends, Nick, who was talking about his Chinese girlfriend. I was teaching an English class at the university, and she was a student in my class. Mom wrote: "Barry made the connection that she was one of Barry's students that he taught English to, at the University, and mentioned that she was very bright, with good English, and quite pretty. This revelation indicated to me that perhaps I should be a little leery. I am not stupid, and I do not want to go through that again. I talked to my Chinese friend Mei Di and she told me that she knew that Barry really loved me because she had asked him once what was going to happen when we moved back to the US and Barry said that he had hoped that I would live with him. All I know is that I love Barry and for me fidelity is innate. I don't want to question our relationship, but I have been deceived before. The next day, my 'suspicions' were totally wrong. Barry wanted to know what was up with me and I told him my worries . . . he reassured me. I have resolved to trust once again."

Though I never really had a serious girlfriend before, I had never been a "player," always going out with only one woman at a time. I also was tainted, coming from a divorced home. I loved Mom and also had no interest in any kind of drama or, for sure, any other woman. Understandably, it took Mom a while to relearn how to trust.

Mom and I took a quick, three-day trip by plane from Kunming to Beijing, so Mom could see China's most important and capital city before she returned to the US. Mom wrote: "I like Beijing. The streets are wide, clean. The people seemed more relaxed than Kunming-ren. There is more physical diversity to the city and cultural diversity. Barry took me to the Hilton for dinner where they had a special 'Pacific Northwest menu.' The dinner was very good and afterwards we met up with some of Barry's J.P. Morgan associates for drinks and karaoke (I once again was 'forced' into participating in this bizarre form of Asian entertainment)."

On May 8, 1995, Mom wrote: "Travels in China are coming to a close. I said goodbye to Barry this afternoon until we meet again in San Francisco, in the beginning of August. I cried when we said our farewells. I think because in part it signified the closure of this trip, which has been magnificent. China is like no other place on earth . . . it has resisted Western influence for so long until recently. Now capitalism is rampant and Western products are popping up everywhere. But there is an attitude here in the people that is clearly Chinese . . . and although I am a bit bored of Kunming, I will miss China and I hope to return within a few years."

Being with some of my J.P. Morgan colleagues in Beijing made me think seriously about work for the first time during my travels. By then, it had been almost five months since I had worked at J.P. Morgan in Singapore—and had received a paycheck. The truth was that I was not bored in the least living the simple existence in a $10-a-day dorm room with Mom, studying Mandarin, learning firsthand about China, its unprecedented rise out of poverty, and its completely undeveloped state. I had remembered, only four years earlier, traveling through Western China with my friend Mei, seeing literally thousands of Chinese workers building a road with only shovels, something that would be relatively easy today with a few excavators. Although I respected Mom's decision to leave Kunming, particularly given that she had come to China for me, and it was not her priority to go there in the first place, I was not yet finished with the experience. Nor was I, honestly, itching to get back to work.

Mom also wrote one short entry about volunteering in an orphanage weekly in Kunming: "There is one child I spend most of my time with . . . just holding him because he appears to be in incredible pain. He is probably about 4, but his body and weight are like that of an infant. His face is flaky and scabbed. His head is abnormally shaped. I feed him (via bottle). I have to pull his lips down for him to suck the bottle. It is a struggle feeding him because inevitably he bites his lip and it bleeds. So usually I just hold him which seems to pacify him a bit." I could tell the days when Mom came back from volunteering at the orphanage. It definitely weighed heavily on her, particularly the fact that 90% of the orphans were female because of China's one-child policy and the Chinese preference for sons over daughters.

This was Mom's last entry on our China adventure: "My last night in Kunming, there was a going-away party for me. It was a great evening and we drank a lot of Chinese beer. I said farewell to everyone . . . kissed all the Italians, hugged the rest. The sun is rising now in Singapore and I feel content. Today I am going home. My wonderful journey that started six months ago is ending, and it is time to start reorganizing my life. I have so much gratitude in my heart for Barry because he truly changed my life. I hope that we will prove to be compatible back in the US and also hope he'll love Gryphen."

As you know, Mom loved Gryphen deeply. She had been with Mom through the good times and bad times, and now good times again, though Gryphen was staying with Grandma and Grandpa, who took amazing care of her. Mom talked all the time about Gryphen. She even developed some repeatable phrases in Mandarin to launch into talking about Gryphen with anyone who would listen. It was usually endearing but sometimes annoying!

Mom surprised Grandma and Grandpa, arriving home on the Friday before Mother's Day. Grandma said, "When the doorbell rang, my heart skipped a beat. There stood Jackie, our adventurous daughter. She said, 'Happy Mother's Day, Mom!' Believe me, it was one of my happiest Mother's Days. She looked so happy and content! She told us all about her traveling adventures and her traveling companion, Barry."

I had planned to stay in China until August, after about a month without Mom, but I decided that it was time for me, too, to head home. I did love the China experience, but without Mom there, it was not the same. I had lived such an independent life and never really got used to being around someone so much. Without Mom in the dorm and cruising around Kunming, I felt that it might be time to return home too. My responsible brain told me that perhaps I should transition back to my career, even though I had told J.P. Morgan that I

Gryphen, 1995

was taking a one-year sabbatical. My initial goal was to become fluent in Mandarin, which I had begun studying in Singapore several years before. Though my Mandarin did get good enough for me to write a few thousand characters and converse comfortably, I was nowhere close to my fluency goal. However, something so much more important had happened. I had the most unexpected and amazing six-month adventure with Mom, which started as a friendship and turned into what was to be the only love of my life.

This brings me back to the phrase "You can only connect the dots afterwards." It is great to pursue goals, have a plan, and so on, but very often the most unexpectedly positive things can happen if one is willing to be open to them! Up until that point, I was really not sure if I would ever find a special partner to share my life with. Mom and I had learned so much about each other by being together so intensely for such a long period, sharing so many amazing experiences, meeting so many interesting people, seeing some incredible sights, relying on and being able to trust each other. As I have said, that trip was so consequential in my life. I have been blessed to have been able to experience that and what resulted from that, including the both of you.

Before that trip, I was so dedicated to and loved my work. J.P. Morgan transferred me from one country to the next almost yearly. While this was also a great period in my life, I knew something was missing, and then Mom came along. I just don't know what direction my life would have taken had Mom not entered my life at that point. Honestly, as painful as it is to now contemplate being without Mom for the rest of my life, it is equally painful to contemplate never having had Mom in my life. I can tell you that I would not have had a fraction of the joy, contentment, love, and peace that I have had—even with the tragedy of losing dear Mom. I know that I have truly been blessed.

Durian: Love it or hate it, this s
t is a favourite with Singaporeans
ople find the smell of
d indeed
HELVETIA
28-8-95
Nr. 76 Aufnahme und Verlag: Hans Schmocker, Lau
Lyell + DIANE Holme
5 FALLING LEAF
IRVINE, CA 92
USA
leaving for London on Sunday.
I miss you both. It was so nice
to have you up in San Francisco
for a few days. How's Gryphen?
Give her a hug + kiss from me. Love,
to glandular impl
violent tendency
for it at times.
to travel alone through any part
the planet I chose
harassed
Far East Plaza
Hyatt Regency
Mount Elizabeth Hospital
MOUNT ELIZABETH LINK
CAIRNHILL
Cairnhill Place
Thong Sia Building
Wellington Building
Pacific Plaza
Scotts
Al-Falah

6

Transition to Sausalito, then Moving to London: Round 1 (June 1995)

I had purchased a house in Sausalito in 1991 when I was living in Singapore. Mom had stayed with me in that house, when we were just friends in early November 1994. So we had a great place to go back to. I remember, while I was still in China, speaking on the phone to Mom in early June of 1995, after she returned to California. She told me that she was going to travel up north to the Bay Area to visit Marci and Brian. Mom and I had been very closely together for six months and knew all about each other's family, but this was the first time either one of us had met the other's family member. I used this occasion to decide to leave China early and surprise Mom. I missed her presence in my daily life greatly. This was a very new experience for me. After living together 24/7 for close to six months, we had been apart, at that time, for over one month.

The surprise worked perfectly, Mom cried, and it was a nice reunion. We moved into my Sausalito house shortly thereafter, and Mom traveled to Iowa to see Julie and the rest of Mom's family there. She left me the following letter: "Dearest Barry, I'll spare you from my urge to be syrupy Romantic in this letter but you have to indulge me when I return and let me lavish a little affection on you, because I miss you and love you immensely. . . . and I will promise to cull my Iowa stories to a few short monologues, ok? Did you happen to ask Toba or Marci about a vacuum cleaner? I also think it would be advantageous to get an additional phone line downstairs for the computer. [We were dealing with dial-up internet in those days.] Did you happen to check out 'grills' as opposed to 'girls'? Please look at gas or electric. I have included a list of movies you might want to watch, as you may have a little time on your hands when Houston beats

303 South Street, Sausalito, California, 1995

Orlando in the NBA finals tomorrow night. Please don't spend all your time at Kinkos! Of course, you have to see *Lawrence of Arabia*, but please don't watch it without me! Love, Jackie."

It is funny to think that only two months earlier Mom and I were having these crazy once-in-a-lifetime adventures and then all of a sudden Mom was writing me about mundane domestic duties like a vacuum cleaner and electric versus gas grill. We had become so domestic in such a short time that Mom told her friend Karen her pet peeve: "Barry uses so much dish-washing soap when he washes dishes." This was a strange, new adventure for me. During those days Mom and I decided that we would give it a go living in Sausalito together while I decided whether I wanted to go back to J.P. Morgan, working in the financial markets. We knew that this would likely entail moving back overseas.

Mom and I decided to have a small family gathering, so Grandma and Grandpa drove up north so our families could meet. Papa Dave and Grandma Shirley, Baba Toba, Marci, Brian, and cousins Gloria, Brock, and Florence were there. As Grandma said, "Everyone was so pleasant and kind and all spoke so highly of Jackie." At that point, Mom was considering applying to nursing school and was keen on getting a job at a doctor's office, to get some practical experience, which she promptly did.

Sausalito, California

As for me, I had not lived in the United States since 1987 and in California since 1983, so I was enjoying the reintroduction to life in the US/CA while living with Mom in a place I loved, Sausalito. There were definitely some adjustments to life together in Sausalito, one being that we were no longer traveling but actually living in my house with both of our lives still a bit unsettled. However, we took that in stride.

As I had never lived in Sausalito and had visited the town for only brief periods, I really did not know anyone in Northern California other than Marci and Brian, my cousins Gloria and Brock in Mill Valley, and Florence and her family who lived in the South Bay. Reading the *Wall Street Journal* one day at what was then Café Soleil (and today is Caffe DiVino) in Sausalito, I saw an advertisement from USAID calling for people with financial expertise to volunteer in developing countries. The average posting was for two to four weeks. That seemed perfect—I would remain mentally engaged, travel to some new places, and still have plenty of time with Mom in Sausalito.

My first posting was in Vladivostok, eastern Russia. I purchased some tapes and started to study elementary Russian. I did not know it then, but that trip cemented my interest in Russia, the Russian language, and the incredible transition Russia was going through. Mom and I grew up when the Soviet Union, dominated by Russia, was the only major rival/enemy of the United States. There was the constant fear of a nuclear event between our two countries. This threat was now gone, and Russia was in the midst of one of the world's most historic transitions. I wanted to be involved somehow!

I enjoyed the experience in Vladivostok immensely. After about a month back in Sausalito, I was asked to go to Bishkek, Kyrgyzstan, to advise the central bank of the country on setting up a proper foreign exchange market. Kyrgyzstan was one of the five "-stans" of the former Soviet Union in Central Asia. Having read almost all of Peter Hopkirk's books on Central Asia, including *The Great Game* a few times, this was like a dream come true, particularly the opportunity to do some mountain climbing in Kyrgyzstan, a beautiful country with some of the world's best, and unknown, climbing.

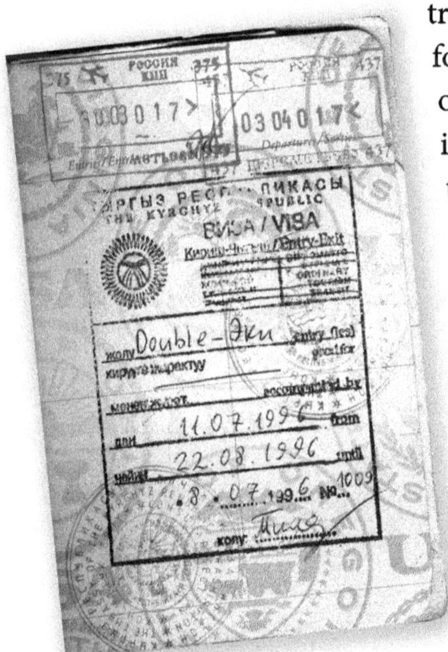

Bishkek was very exciting for me! It was very much still stuck in the former Soviet Union, but with an amazing backdrop of majestic, snow-capped mountains. I loved the cultural balance between Russian-looking people and Central Asian cultures. After my second week on the job, there was a three-day weekend and I used this opportunity to hire a guide and try to climb one of the mountains named Uchitel (teacher) in the Pamir Mountain range. On the second day we summited the mountain, and it definitely "taught" me something as I had a bad fall and broke my ankle.

At first, my guide said he would leave me at our tent and go back to get help. I rejected that option as we were in the middle of nowhere. In the end, it was a ten-hour walk back with me hopping on one foot, leaning on my guide's shoulder all the way to his car. We had to leave all of our equipment where we had camped the night before. I made contact with the representatives of USAID, who were adamant about my going to Almaty, Kazakhstan, a four-hour drive from Bishkek, to get X-rayed, as they had more confidence in the hospital there than the one in Bishkek. I was not 100% sure whether it was a bad sprain or a break at that point.

It turned out that I did break my ankle, which meant getting a cast on, crutches, and so on. I also had to stay in Almaty for close to a week because I was not in any condition for a long flight—more than thirty-six hours—back to the US. Despite this mishap, I can definitely say that I was now "hooked" on Russia and the former Soviet republics, particularly the five "-stans" (Kazakhstan, Turkmenistan, Uzbekistan, Tajikistan, and Kyrgyzstan).

It might seem strange that I had been so interested in China and was even willing to devote a good part of my sabbatical to living in China and studying Mandarin but then was willing to put aside China in favor of Russia and the former Soviet republics. However, the part of China that most fascinated me was the western Silk Road area that leads to the "-stans" through which Genghis Khan and the Mongol hordes had invaded Europe, where Marco Polo had made his legendary trip to China, and where the "Great Game" conflict between Russia and England in the 1800s took place. In those days, I had committed myself to traveling the length of the Silk Road, in stages, from Beijing to its important terminus, Baku in Azerbaijan, and finished this journey only last year, 2018, after multiple trips since 1994, some with Mom.

My experiences with USAID led, later on, to our family spending our first years together in Moscow, Russia. Though I did not tell Mom then not wanting to scare her, I knew I would somehow find a good job opportunity in Russia and was awaiting that possibility.

It was great to return from Central Asia to Mom in Sausalito. Mom was enjoying her work at a doctor's office and applying to nursing school. At that point, I think I had had enough adventure and, after speaking with J.P. Morgan and some ex-colleagues who had moved to another bank (Chemical Bank, which soon became Chase Bank), I felt that I needed to get back to work.

J.P. Morgan wanted to send me to Buenos Aires, Argentina, on a three-year posting. I had lived in Buenos Aires in 1986 and, despite enjoying that experience and making some long-term Argentine friends, I did not want to go back and live there for three years. I said to myself, "Been there, done that." My ex-J.P. Morgan colleagues, now at Chemical Bank, proposed that I join Chemical Bank in London as managing director responsible for emerging markets, including Eastern Europe and Russia. Given my newfound interest in Russia, this was an easy decision, though it was tough to leave J.P. Morgan where I had spent ten great years, launched my career, earned reasonable money, made some lifelong friends, and lived around the world.

In the end, I had lived and worked in six different countries in my ten years with J.P. Morgan. Now I had to sit down with Mom and have a talk. Although we loved each other a lot, and I could not possibly see myself with anyone else, neither of us had felt that it was time to get married. We had not actually discussed it, but it was something we each understood. I knew Mom wanted to go to nursing school. I also knew that if I wanted to stay in my industry, I could not let too much time go by before getting back to work in finance. Mom said that she was very willing to move with me to London, and I promised that, at the end of the three-year guaranteed contract with Chemical Bank, we would prioritize what we would do next according to her interests.

Moving to London, Round No. 1, Together (1995)

Up until that point, one of my favorite places in the world was Gimmelwald, Switzerland. I was first there in 1978 with my friend Steve when we backpacked through Europe after graduating from high school. I had taken many friends and family there, even Baba Toba, over the years. When I lived in Zurich for one year (1991 to '92), I visited Gimmelwald many times. Thus, before arriving in London, which would be our home for roughly the next year, Mom and I decided to spend a few extra days hiking in the Berner Oberland. It was a wonderful trip, and we would go back a few times as a family. You may remember a really nice summer trip there with the whole family and with Valentina and her

A postcard from Gimmelwald, Switzerland, 1995

children. Benjamin, you tricked Mom into a bet that she would give you money if you found a snake, which we had already found and were hiding from her.

Mom sent a postcard to Grandma and Grandpa on August 24, 1995, from Gimmelwald: "Dear Mom and Dad, We made it to Switzerland! It is so beautiful here in Gimmelwald, as you can see from the front of the postcard. Today, Barry and I took a hike . . . it was a bit rainy but still quite heavenly. Before we drove here to the mountains, we spent a few hours in Zurich and Barry showed me where he used to live. Surprisingly, it was just down the street from where Vladimir Lenin lived as a refugee before he returned to Russia to launch

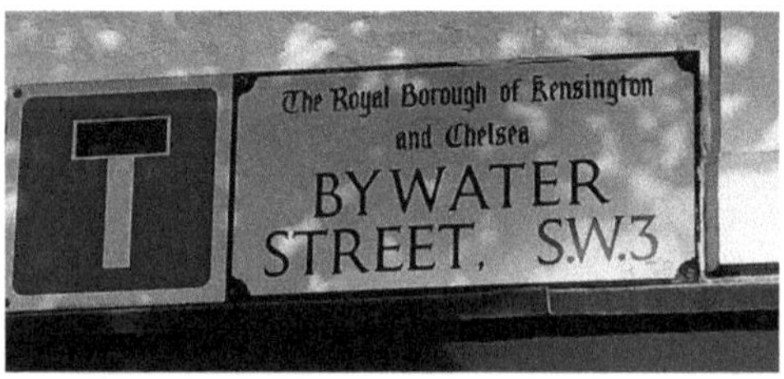

Bywater Street, Chelsea, London, 1995

the Russian Revolution in 1917. Zurich is very charming and we're going back there on Saturday and leaving for London on Sunday. I miss you both. It was so nice to have you up in San Francisco for a few days. How's Gryphen? Give her a hug and kiss from me. Love, Jackie."

I remember arriving at a very cute hotel in London, 11 Cadogan Gardens near Sloane Square. 11 Cadogan Gardens was built in the nineteenth century by Lord Chelsea. We arrived late on a Saturday night, and I remember waking up the next morning to the news, on CNN, that Chemical Bank and Chase Manhattan Bank had announced a merger. I found out the next day, my first day at work, that my job responsibility for the foreseeable future was to manage the firing of a good number of my staff that I had not even met. It was August 1995. I had a guaranteed three-year contract for a very large sum of money. Part of me tried to motivate myself to stick it out, collect the money, and then do what we wanted to do. Mom and I had a wonderful little house in Chelsea and we had a nice lifestyle, although we did not know a lot of people in London at that point.

What always impressed me about Mom was her ability to adapt to new environments with her cheery attitude, enjoying every day and making new friends easily. Mom and I would often spend a weekend day in London, strolling around the Piccadilly area, going to a movie and then to Wagamama, which was our favorite place to eat. Mom loved to go to the movies. She would often look in the movie guides to see if her very favorite movie of all time, *Lawrence of Arabia*, was playing. I think we probably saw *Lawrence of Arabia* on the big screen in London at least three or four times. Also, very often, in the evening on my way home from work, Mom and I would meet to work out at a gym we belonged to and then eat at a restaurant, Orielles, on Sloane Square for dinner and a glass of wine. We had a nice visit from my niece Kathryn, Marci, and Baba Toba while we were living in Chelsea.

Much as I tried, it took me a couple of months to realize that my heart was not into my new job. I had developed some serious stomach problems, likely a legacy of life in China, and the anxiety caused by having to fire people didn't help matters.

I remember, like it was yesterday, being in a pub in Chelsea, London, with Mom and seeing a woman with a Lonely Planet Africa book. That night, over beers and fish and chips, Mom and I hatched a plan for me to quit my job and travel through Africa overland from Nairobi, Kenya, to Cape Town, South Africa. Obviously neither Mom nor I had gotten "adventure" out of our systems. I remember Mom and me spending quite a few days roaming around the London embassies of numerous African countries such as Kenya, Tanzania, Malawi, Mozambique, Zimbabwe, Zambia, Namibia, Botswana, and South Africa, getting visas for our trip to save us a lot of time during our travels. While we were in London, though, we did take a number of great trips to different places, including Scotland, Venice, Paris, and the Czech Republic.

Mom wrote in a postcard, from Prague, to Grandma and Grandpa on November 22, 1995: "Dear Mom and Dad, Barry and I arrived in Prague today. . . . Barry went to business meetings and I went wandering around the city. Prague is the most beautiful city I've ever seen. I spent the day wandering around the

PRAHA
VLTAVA A PRAŽSKÝ HRAD

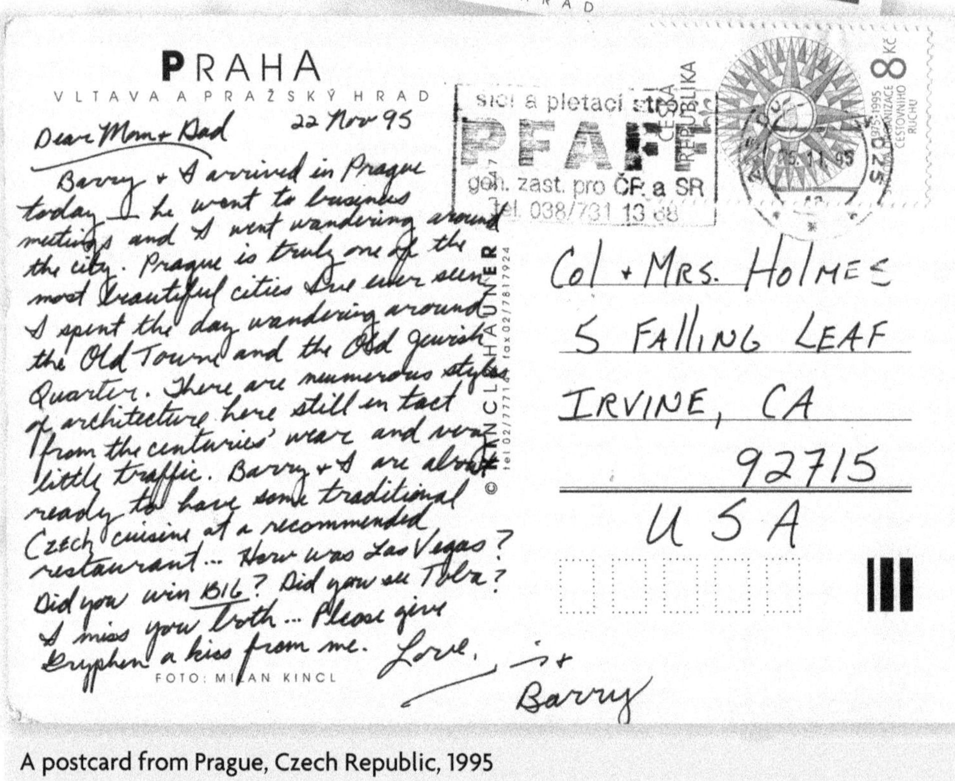
PRAHA
VLTAVA A PRAŽSKÝ HRAD
22 Nov 95
Dear Mom + Dad
Barry + I arrived in Prague today. He went to business meetings and I went wandering around the city. Prague is truly one of the most beautiful cities I've ever seen. I spent the day wandering around the Old Town and the Old Jewish Quarter. There are numerous styles of architecture here still in tact from the centuries' wear and very little traffic. Barry + I are about ready to have some traditional Czech cuisine at a recommended restaurant... How was Las Vegas? Did you win BIG? Did you see Tolz? I miss you both... Please give Gryphon a kiss from me. Love,
+ Barry
FOTO: MILAN KINCL
© KINCL HAUNER tel 02/7771... fax 02/7817924
šicí a pletací stroje
PFAFF
gen. zast. pro ČR a SR
tel. 038/731 13 88
ČESKÁ REPUBLIKA
8 Kč
CESTOVNÍHO RUCHU
Col + Mrs. Holmes
5 Falling Leaf
Irvine, CA
92715
USA

A postcard from Prague, Czech Republic, 1995

Old Town and the Old Jewish Quarter. There are numerous styles of architecture here still intact from the centuries' wear and tear and very little traffic. Barry and I are about ready to have some traditional Czech cuisine at a recommended restaurant. . . . How was Las Vegas? Did you win *BIG*? Did you see Toba? Miss you both. . . . Please give Gryphen a kiss from me. Love, Jackie and Barry." Before Mom and I left London, we took a trip north to Scotland for New Year's. We loved Scotland, the ruggedness, the scenery, the people. I remember attempting a fun pub crawl in Edinburgh where you are supposed to drink a pint at each pub along some main street. We started out in the first two pubs with pints and soon were asking for their smallest glass of beer, which elicited a bit of good-humored ribbing from the bartenders.

After I returned to London, it was a bit stressful for me our last week because I was leaving a very lucrative job and my career again after only about five months. Was it something about my career that I did not particularly like? Was it the circumstances? Or was it the allure of adventure with a willing travel partner whom I loved? Likely it was all three. However, I did feel a bit of guilt in letting down the people who hired me. I know it was not a good reflection in the eyes of senior management at Chemical/Chase Bank that I was quitting. Although I did feel a bit like a quitter, my heart told me that I was doing the right thing, and it had not failed me recently, both in taking the sabbatical from J.P. Morgan and in asking Mom to travel on with me to China. Up until those decisions, I thought more cerebrally about my career, the right thing to do, the path forward in life, and so forth. Using my heart to help guide my decisions was something new, and as I look back, it certainly worked.

TANZANIA
24.03.96
TANZANIA
© Copy Right. S. CHOMOCO. P.O. Box 1324, ARUSHA.
3/24/96
Col. + Mrs. Holme
5 Falling L
Irvine, CA
927
USA
AAC135

7

The Big African Adventure, Overland from Nairobi to Cape Town (March 1996)

It was early March 1996. The first thing we noticed after landing in Nairobi was the contrast between our white skin (after a winter in London) and the black skin of the Kenyans. We remarked that "we looked like ghosts!" Mom and I spent a few days in Nairobi getting used to the environment before heading to the Meru province of Kenya, where I had planned to climb Mount Kenya. Unfortunately, my camera broke the first day of the trip, so we have no pictures of the amazing adventure in Africa that was about to commence, but we do have many entries from dear Mom's diary.

Here is Mom's description of Nairobi: "The city from the start didn't grab me (as Barry came up with the right expression for me). First nothing appeared beautiful or eye-catching, except for the mosque, no significant architecture, no gardens or trees, only nondescript buildings. It took us a full day to get grounded in Kenya/Africa. I could see that Barry was a bit on guard as well. But I think we are both comfortable now about the safety factor. I find it difficult here, though, to get involved in a good old conversation with the locals. The exception was at Buffalo Bills, a bar at our hotel. We were in there for no more than two minutes when several pretty young black women came up to us. I spoke with Rose and Julie for about ¾ of an hour about life in Nairobi. Julie had just broken up with her boyfriend 5 days ago and wanted to know if Barry ever came home late, what he was like as a boyfriend, what men were like in general in the US. Barry had a lengthy conversation with an older gentleman about the history and politics of Kenya." Again, I was always amazed how Mom would meet random people from all walks of life, and within a very short period they were telling her the most personal details of their lives.

The next day, we were off to Mount Kenya. Mom was such a trooper, even hiking part of the way with me. I remember Mom feeling a bit bad when I told her that I did not think it was the best idea for her to try to climb Mount Kenya all the way to the top with me. I was in the best shape of my life and ready for the challenge and Mom had not prepared, in London, to do any climbing. I was still learning how to be a good partner, and, in hindsight, I should have engaged her about training and climbing with me while we were in London. My bad, lesson learned.

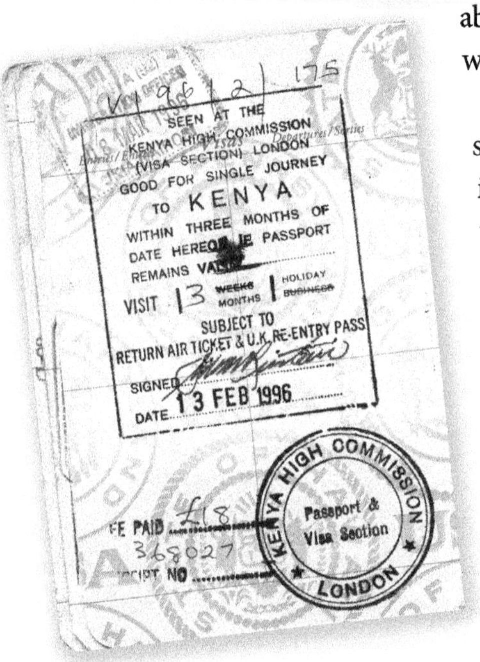

Before summiting Mount Kenya, we spent a wonderful evening in our cabin with a full Scottish Army brigade that was in training on the mountain. Mom's first entry in the Africa section of her diary, on March 13, 1996, read: "Mountain Rock Hotel, near Nanyuki, Kenya . . . Barry and I came here so that he could climb Mt. Kenya, which is where he is still at, hopefully on his descent from the summit as I'm writing this. I climbed (actually hiked uphill) with him to the Old Moses hut at 3,200 meters on the Sirimon Route where we stopped for the night. We spent the night with 16 members of the Scottish Battalion, a German named Rolf and our guide Elijah, from the Kikuyu tribe. The next morning, I hiked part of the way with Barry. The air felt so good in my lungs. I don't know where all my energy was coming from. I walked back to Old Moses with my guide and passed all of the Scots and cheered them on . . . a nice group of guys. I walked with three people from South Africa who had summited Mt. Kenya the night before. I've yet to meet a young South African I haven't liked. The next morning, I met my guide Steven to go horseback riding. It was so much fun doing an actual ride, but very exhausting.

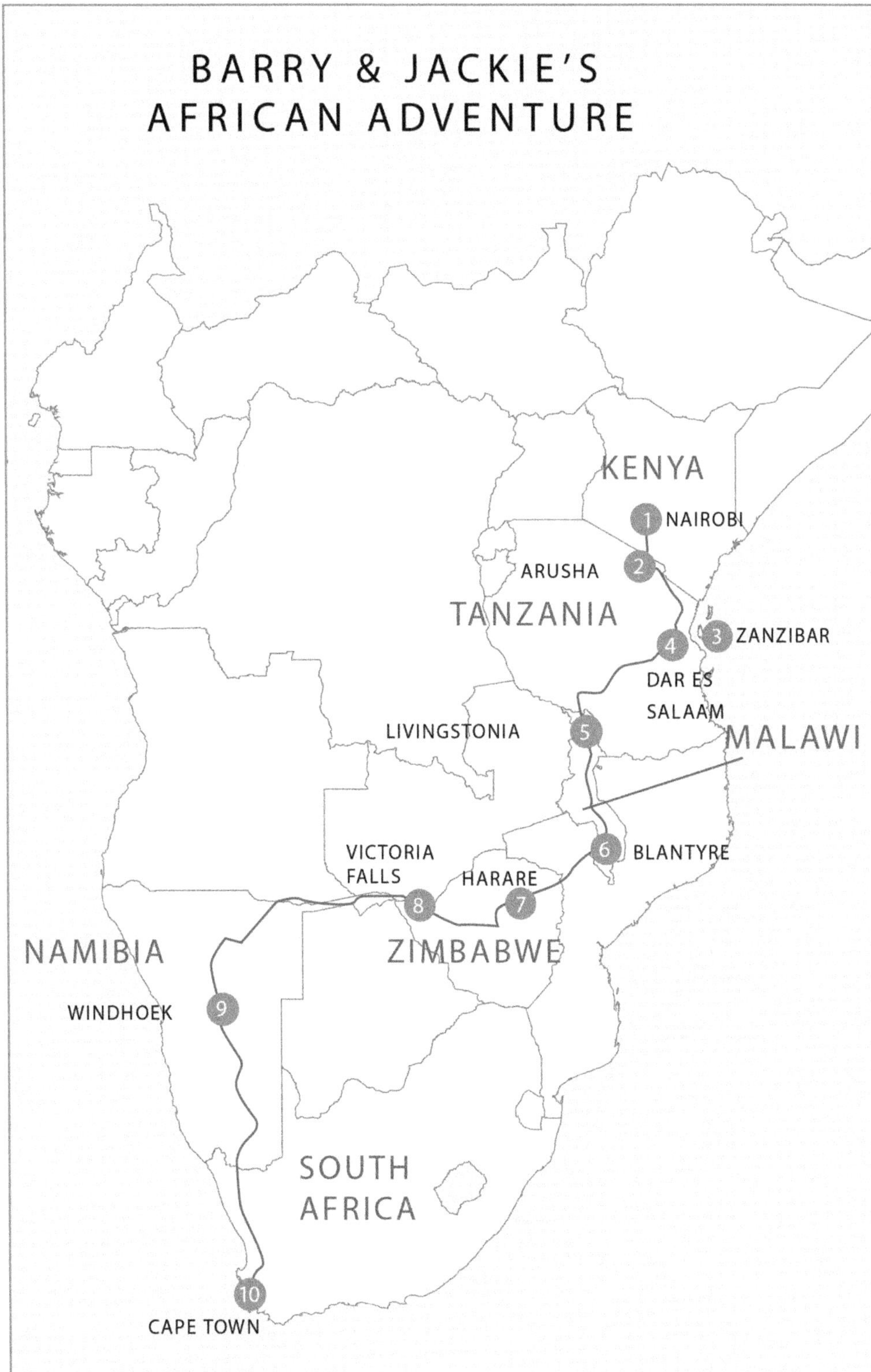
BARRY & JACKIE'S
AFRICAN ADVENTURE
KENYA
1 NAIROBI
2 ARUSHA
TANZANIA
3 ZANZIBAR
4 DAR ES SALAAM
5 LIVINGSTONIA
MALAWI
6 BLANTYRE
VICTORIA FALLS
HARARE
7
8
NAMIBIA
ZIMBABWE
9 WINDHOEK
SOUTH AFRICA
10 CAPE TOWN

Barry said he would be back today, but I hope he ends up staying another night on the mountain because I think descending from the summit all the way down in one day is way too exhausting."

After Mount Kenya, next up was a safari and then Mount Kilimanjaro. Mom's entry from that day, March 19, 2016, was: "Barry and I took the Arusha Express bus to Arusha. We rode with many Kenyans and Tanzanians and a few Westerners. The scenery was great and increasingly lush as we approached Arusha, passing villages and Maasai shepherds with cattle and goats here and there. As we drove towards town, we watched with awe what we thought was Mt. Kilimanjaro, but actually learned later it was Mt. Meru."

We had started to be a lot more comfortable in "our shoes" being in and traveling around Africa. It took us a while as we were used to the ease with which one can travel in Asia compared with the challenges of traveling overland in Africa.

Before heading off to Kilimanjaro, we decided to do a safari. As Mom wrote: "We set off on our safari on March 17th and the first animals we saw were giraffes, 3 of them very close to our vehicle. I could have watched them all day, they were so graceful. They reminded me of dinosaurs, I'm sure because of their height. Their eyes are like cow-eyes and when they run, it's as if they are part of a broken dream, moving so slowly. We came across several Maasai people, most of them tending their herds of goats and cattle. They are so striking because at a distance you can spot them in their bright red garments . . . draped over their shoulders and wrapped about them. To see them against the lush green backdrop of the African plain near the Ngorongoro Crater is amazing . . . the contrast of red, green, blue sky, white clouds and their herds of brown, white, black, gray cattle & goats. The third night we camped on the rim of the crater. The view was spectacular, and we had a thunderstorm in our camp in the afternoon. During the night, you could hear, from our tent, zebras grazing (and Barry snoring which I was sure would attract all sorts of beasts). As for the Serengeti, the wildebeest migration was vast . . . for as far as your eye could see there were wildebeest covering the plains of the Serengeti. But what was really amazing was seeing the great migration of the zebras. They are so odd

Zebras, Tanzania, 1996

looking . . . so artificial in many ways, so wild and the strange black-and-white-striped patterns. The baby zebra are most fun to watch because their movements are so sporadic and energetic."

I remember telling Mom how strange life is that eighteen months earlier I was only occasionally in contact with her as friends. Then, in what seemed like the flick of an instant, we were together, traveling through India, Laos, Thailand, and Burma, living and studying in China for four months, living in Sausalito together for a while, moving to and living in London, and now going on a safari in Africa—like a lifetime of togetherness, adventures, and memories packed into eighteen months.

We camped that first night on the plains of the Serengeti. What an experience! Mom wrote: "The first night we camped in the Serengeti, we heard hyenas in our camp and in fact Barry and I saw them when we began walking to the toilet. Barry was aiming the flashlight down the trail and we saw the reflection of several eyes. The next morning, early, there was a single male water buffalo grazing in our camp. They are one of the most dangerous animals to come across, and Barry wanted to walk by it . . . the buffalo looked straight at us as we were about to walk by, saying 'don't even think about it.' We didn't challenge it and walked immediately back. A large family of baboons was very busy going through the garbage in our camp. A couple of females came by carrying their babies. A very young baboon came up close to me curiously, then when I bent down it freaked and began screaming. . . . A couple of bigger baboons came immediately by and I cowered behind Barry who scared them off by stomping his foot and raising his voice. We saw many animals in the Serengeti. The first lion we came across was a female who was sunning behind a rock. Not long after that we came across a male and female obviously courting. The second day in the Serengeti we saw wildebeests, ostriches, Kori-bustards, more gazelles, zebras, lions, warthogs, and bat-eared foxes. Bat-eared foxes are *very* cute. The big event of the day was the sighting of a cheetah, my favorite big cat and the one I respect the most. She was lean and beautiful and kept her eye on the zebras which were everywhere. About 100 meters behind her were two female hyenas ready to steal her kill. By the 4th day we had had enough of confinement in a vehicle, and it hampered our enthusiasm for sighting animals. Barry was particularly 'dulled.' But in retrospect, the safari was magnificent, and I will always remember and relish the experience."

I don't want to sound like a spoiled, unappreciative traveler. I did love seeing the animals. I do have to admit, however, at that time I more enjoyed the physical exertion of mountain climbing, seeing new places, and connecting with the locals.

One of the worst places we had to pass through in our travels was Arusha, Kenya. By this year, in 2019, I have traveled to over 125 countries and can say that our experience in Arusha and my experience at the border of Benin and Nigeria, trying to cross overland in 2017, are two of the worst I have had traveling in my life. I remember arriving in Arusha by bus from Nairobi and all the lowlifes at the bus station trying to scam us. We ended up getting scammed out of half of a $400 deposit we left with a "travel company" for the Kilimanjaro climb.

Mom's description was livelier: "When we arrived at the bus station in Arusha, we were 'attacked' by over a dozen black men pushing their safari tours on us and offering rides to our hotel. It was totally overwhelming, and I could not shake them. Finally, there appeared a rather large older man with a very deep voice shooing the others away and offering to take us to our hotel. His name was Clemence Munta."

The name of his "company" was Star Tours. It turned out that he was ultimately the man who scammed us, as Mom said: "A name that will live in infamy in our Arusha adventure. That night at dinner, after booking our Kilimanjaro trip with Clemence and Star Tours, and the morning before leaving for our safari, we ate dinner at a restaurant and spoke with some Germans who, it turned out, were on the same safari with us the next day. They told us that they were going to book with Star Tours but had been told that many people were getting ripped off."

Mom wrote: "Barry and I started laughing, realizing that we were indeed ripped off as well. After dinner, we stopped by the police station to lodge a complaint. Barry spoke for us at the police station, 'I'd like to ask you something . . . have you heard of a company called Star Tours and a man named Clemence?' All 20 of the policemen at the station looked up and one man said, 'Yes. He is here in lock-up. Would you like to see him?' Barry said, 'Yes.' So they brought Clemence out who now looked rather disheveled with shirt hanging out of his pants, sweat on his face, and dirt on his clothes. Barry then said to Clemence's face, 'You're a liar and a cheat, you steal people's money, you scam them, you should be ashamed of yourself. You make a bad name for Arusha and I want my money back!' In the end, we returned to the police station after our Kili trip and got back half of our deposit."

Now we were off to Mount Kilimanjaro, and after climbing Mount Kenya, I was greatly looking forward to another physical challenge, particularly after sitting in a vehicle for four days on our safari. The approach to Kili was about four

Mt. Kilimanjaro, Kenya, 1996

or five days of hiking, and Mom decided that, though she did not feel prepared for the climb, she would accompany me on the first few days.

Mom's entry on March 23, 1996, read: "*Mt. Kilimanjaro!* Mt. Kilimanjaro is what I expected in beauty and attraction. The hike through the forest was lush and mountain wildflowers were still in bloom here and there. We saw several colobus monkeys jumping from tree to tree with their white tails hanging down. I feel a little sad that I won't be going to the top of the mountain as everyone seems very focused on that goal. The mountain is very majestic, and while I know the summit is probably out of my league I would have liked to have continued up the mountain. I understand why people climb mountains . . . there's something very pulling in them, and the feeling of the changes that occur in your body as you ascend is wonderful. The hikes I did with Barry on Mt. Kenya and Mt. Kilimanjaro were some of the best because my body felt so good."

We started our summit climb at midnight, and it was a good bit of work climbing steep scree, but in the end, most of my group, including me, summited on the Marangu Route. The view from the top was spectacular. I did not stay at the top long before starting my descent because I was freezing cold at 19,340 feet. While it was a bit of work on the last day, the summit day, I can't say that it was one of the harder climbs I have done in my life, particularly given the high elevation. What is most spectacular climbing on Kili is the variation of terrain from one day to the next, passing through at least four completely different landscapes, forest, alpine, lunar, and finally snowcapped.

At that point, Mom and I decided we had a pretty hectic traveling pace and, to slow it down, we traveled to Zanzibar, off the coast of Tanzania, where we spent about four or five days in a tiny little no-frills cabin right on one of the most beautiful beaches I had ever seen. Dinner and lunch were always the same . . . rice and the most tasty barbecued fish I had ever eaten and, of course, beer. Mom and I just were lazy, lying on the beach, reading, and enjoying each other's company.

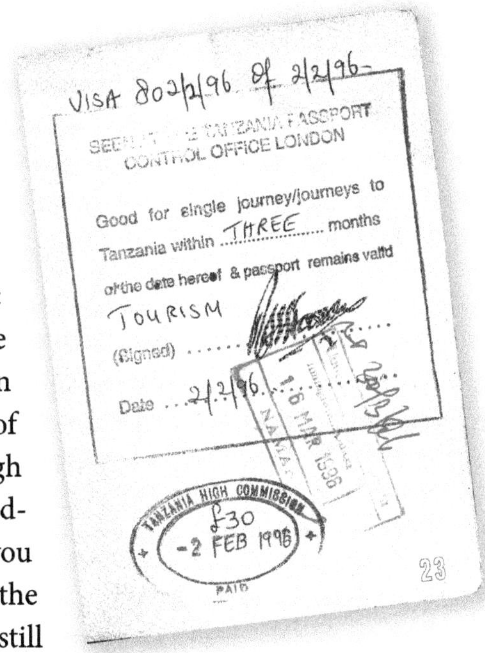

The town of Zanzibar, itself a historic place, was very interesting. Mom and I were in heaven. Mom described Zanzibar: "In Zanzibar the architecture is an influence of Arab and Indian styles. You can walk through narrow streets and see elaborate doors, hand-carved and studded and balconies above you with pointed windows in the back. Most of the buildings are in a state of decay, but they still are beautiful and give the island a sense of cultural aesthetic. Zanzibar is almost entirely Moslem and many of the women wear veils and 'body sacks.'"

Mom continued: "Almost every tourist that comes to Tanzania ends up in Zanzibar, usually at the end of their journey and it seems logical as you want to leave a country on an 'up note,' and the island offers that and redeems Tanzania to an extent. I have found very little about Tanzania and its people that I can praise, regretfully. Throughout my travels in Tanzania I have continually searched for the positive aspects of the culture and I have found almost nothing. The majority seem to be lacking in motivation, intellect, pride and warmth. They are sexist and racist and feel no sense of guilt in failing to honor their word or commitments. I don't believe this is a result of the race but rather the culture of the country. Nonetheless, Tanzania is a beautifully diverse country with Zanzibar, Mt. Meru, Kilimanjaro, the Serengeti, the Ngorongoro Crater, lakes, lush fertile valleys. We have been through the interior of Tanzania and witnessed much of the country's beautiful landscape."

Mom was the least racist and most open-minded person I ever met. These and her many other qualities endeared her to me. However, two things really got on her nerves: chauvinistic/sexist men and very unkind people. Tanzania did seem to have a number of both.

Despite her lack of fondness for the people of Tanzania, Mom still seemed to enjoy her time as evidenced by the postcard she sent to Grandma and Grandpa on March 24, 1996: "Dear Mom and Dad, greetings from Tanzania, Africa! Barry and I were in Kenya for about a week where he climbed Mt. Kenya . . . I hiked up with him part of the way. Right now he is climbing Mt. Kilimanjaro which I just came down from today having just hiked to the first set of huts yesterday and spent the night. The mountain is very beautiful! I'll be on my own in Africa for the next few days while Barry finishes the climb. We'll meet up after his climb and head to the capital of Tanzania, Dar es Salaam ("Home of Peace" in Arabic). We went on a safari before Kilimanjaro and saw *many, many* animals including impalas like the ones on the front of this card. We also saw lions, zebras, wildebeests, giraffes, cheetahs, rhinos, elephants, gazelles, hyenas, etc. . . . but we never saw any animal that was cute as Gryphen. I can't wait to see her and smell her little dog breath. I miss you both very much and hope all is going well for you. Love, Jackie."

Getting back on the traveling circuit after we recharged our batteries in Zanzibar, we traveled through the night from the Tanzanian capital, Dar es Salaam, by train, to the border of Malawi. I remember there being a gap of a few

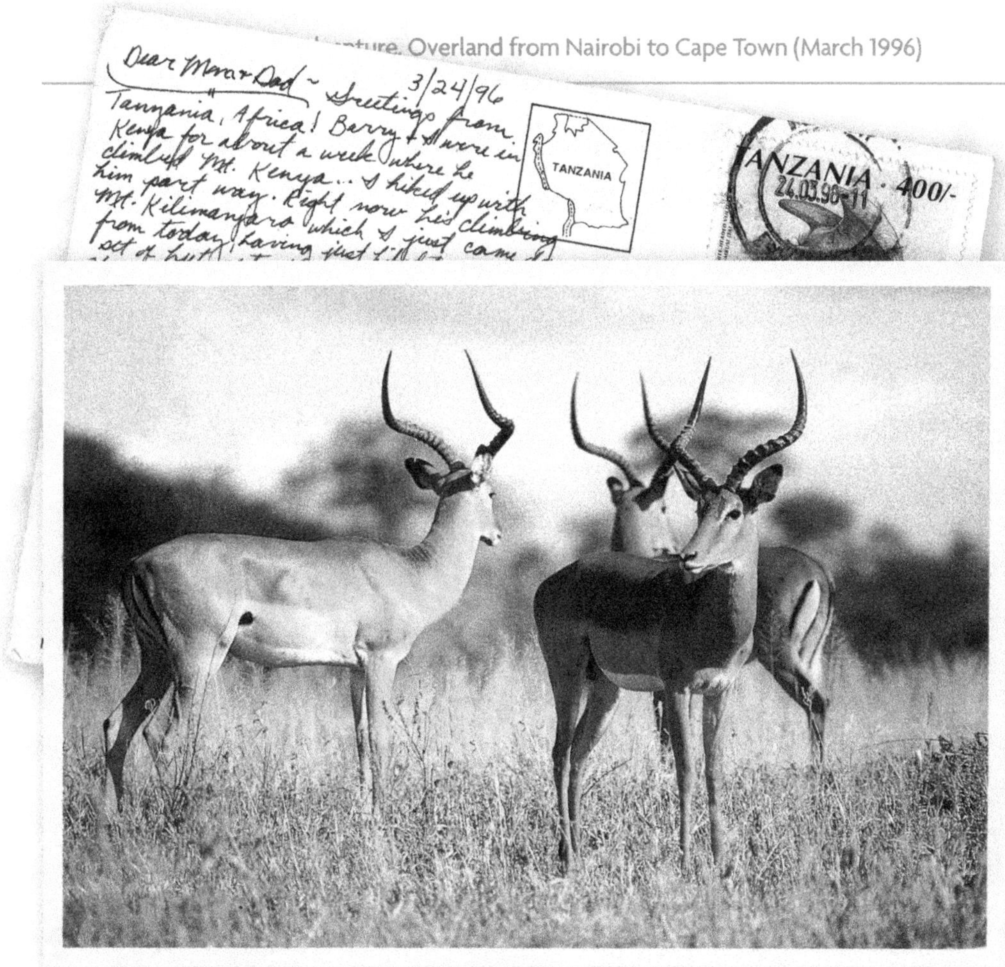

Dear Mom + Dad ~ Greetings from
3/24/96
Tanzania, Africa! Barry + I were in
Kenya for about a week where he
climbed Mt. Kenya... I hiked up with
him part way. Right now he's climbing
Mt. Kilimanjaro which I just came
from today having just
TANZANIA
TANZANIA · 400/-
24.03.96

Postcard from the Serengeti, Tanzania, 1996

miles between the border on the Tanzanian side and the border on the Malawian side. Children, no older than ten, gave us rides on their bikes between the borders, even taking our baggage.

Mom wrote, "Crossing the border from Tanzania to Malawi was comical as we were driven on the back of bicycles (backpacks and all) to the border. Once across, we got on board a truck that continued to pick up passengers until we were sitting on top of people." Sure enough, even in this tense and overcrowded environment crossing the border, Mom wound up chatting and remembering a conversation: "I met a Malawian man who had received his master's from the University of London in East African history and had lectured for seven years at a college on Mt. Kilimanjaro. I asked him which African country had the most potential and he said Botswana, because it had resources and very little conflict between its inhabitants."

Mom and I really liked our introduction to Malawi—definitely off the beaten path, but for us, the gateway from Kenya and Tanzania down to Zimbabwe, Namibia, and South Africa. We could feel right away the difference in how Tanzanians and Malawians treated us, like night and day. Initially, Mom and I had planned to travel straight through the country, but both challenging public transportation schedules and our fondness for Malawi led us to spend a week in the country. We particularly liked Livingstonia, a town founded by missionaries that felt very chill! It was Easter 1996.

Mom wrote: "April 5, 1996, Livingstonia, Malawi. Our introduction to Malawi began with the bus ride from Karonga to Chitimba, the village below Livingstonia. The people on the bus were 'happy,' friendly, smiling and a welcome change from the resentful attitudes of the people of Tanzania. On our 11-hour bus ride to the border of Malawi, we spent 9 hours listening to a black Catholic parish pray the rosary and sing hymns in Swahili. There really was a noticeable change in the people of Malawi vs. those of Tanzania. The people of Malawi seemed much more relaxed, happy, and welcoming to foreigners. We stayed that night in very basic accommodations (no water) and hiked up to Livingstonia in the morning. Before we left, Barry gave John, a 15-year-old boy we met the night before, an old pair of Nike shoes which was a much-appreciated gift judging from his response and the grin on his face. After a couple of nice days at Livingstonia, we waited hours to catch a bus down to Southern Malawi, Nkhata Bay, only to learn that due to Easter, no bus would be forthcoming. We finally climbed on the back of a large pickup truck with about 20 other Malawians."

Next, we were on our way south to Zimbabwe and then

South Africa, catching buses the whole way down. Mom wrote: "The next morning, we caught the early express overnight bus to Harare in Zimbabwe. The bus ride took us through Mozambique which was a beautiful but noticeably poor and underdeveloped country."

We spent a few days in Harare recovering from that long bus ride. Zimbabwe was just in the beginning phases of hyperinflation, owing to the economic and political mismanagement of President Robert Mugabe, which reached into the billions of percentages by 2008. At that time, though, things were still relatively safe and stable for foreigners in Harare, and Mom and I had a few good meals before heading to Vic Falls.

It is interesting to read Mom's entry about our arrival in Harare given all that has happened in Zimbabwe with hyperinflation since Mom and I were there: "As we approached the city of Harare we felt we had left Africa and entered the first world . . . big modern houses with satellite dishes, swimming pools lined the main roads. Well-kept roads, clean streets, and tall buildings marked the city skyline. The level of education amongst the black community also seemed much higher than any other city we had come across in Africa. Buildings were modern and well-kept."

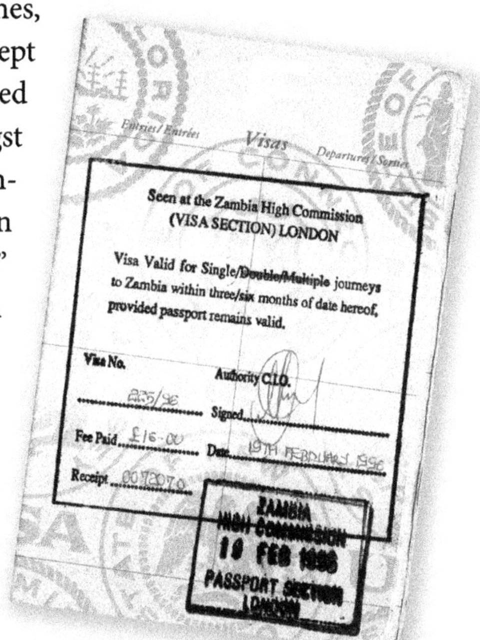

People were helpful and friendly. From Harare we flew to Victoria Falls, the only internal flight we took in Africa. Mom wrote: "The town of Vic Falls was very small but clearly designed for the tourists' convenience. It took all of about 5 minutes to cover the main street. On the Zimbabwe side, the Falls are beautiful. But fortunately, Barry and I had visas to cross over to the Zambian side and *witnessed nature in all of her splendor!* The Falls are breathtaking on the Zambian side . . . very powerful and spectacular. We felt dwarfed by the awesomeness of the Zambezi River falling so forcefully down the sheer cliffs. We stood for a long time admiring the falls and getting drenched from the spray."

Standing right alongside the falls on the Zambian side back then, in 1996, was like watching virtual reality. Elephants roamed right in front of us in the water surrounding the falls, not more than ten to fifteen feet from where Vic Falls plunges hundreds of feet to the Zambezi River. The falls on the Zambian side were so much less populated and were more natural than the falls on the Zimbabwean side. What a combination of power, beauty, and raw nature!

We loved Vic Falls and stayed with a lovely Zimbabwean family that was planning to move to Zambia because of the problems that Mugabe created for "whites." Mom continued: "They had a Great Dane named Otto who was such a pushover and such a good dog! Myra's mother was the quintessential grandmother . . . open-minded, soft spoken but opinionated and very sweet. Myra and Vic were interesting to speak with and gave us quite a bit of insight into the situation in Zimbabwe regarding changes that have occurred as the result of independence and how the white population is leaving, including them. Myra and Vic took Barry and me for a boat ride on the Zambezi River at their boat club and had a couple of beers. What a nice evening!"

Mom ended her entry on Vic Falls with a happy face and this: "Almost every house we passed in Vic Falls had one or two dogs in their yard." We spent two days seeing the falls, which were amazing, particularly with so much animal life roaming around the falls. We also went white-water rafting on the Zambezi. On one of the days we decided to go to the Zambia side of the falls and traveled to Livingstone, Zambia. The taxi dropped us off at a nice hotel that was clearly planning some kind of event for lunch in its outdoor garden. Mom and I asked what the lunch was about and they said the Zambian president, Frederick Chiluba, would be eating there with some friends. Mom and I quickly changed our plans and decided to eat lunch at the hotel, getting a table directly facing theirs. Chiluba took over the presidency from the longtime "dictator-for-life," Kenneth Kaunda. In office for eleven years, Chiluba was the next longest-serving president of Zambia after Kaunda.

It was getting toward mid-April 1996, and Mom and I wanted to make our way down to Cape Town, spending time in Namibia on the way. The only problem was that bus travel south was very unreliable in Vic Falls and the earliest bus was in one week, so we decided to hitchhike our way down. We had a long way to go to get to the capital of Namibia, Windhoek, by my thirty-sixth birthday, on April 16. We needed to travel from Vic Falls in Zimbabwe, past a small section of Botswana, and then across the Caprivi Strip, which separates Zimbabwe, Zambia, Botswana, Angola, and Namibia, and then a good halfway down the length of Namibia. The Caprivi Strip was created in the late 1880s in a swap of territory that gave the Germans, who were present in what is now Namibia, access to the Zambezi River in Zimbabwe/Zambia (then under British rule) in return for Germany dropping its claim to Zanzibar.

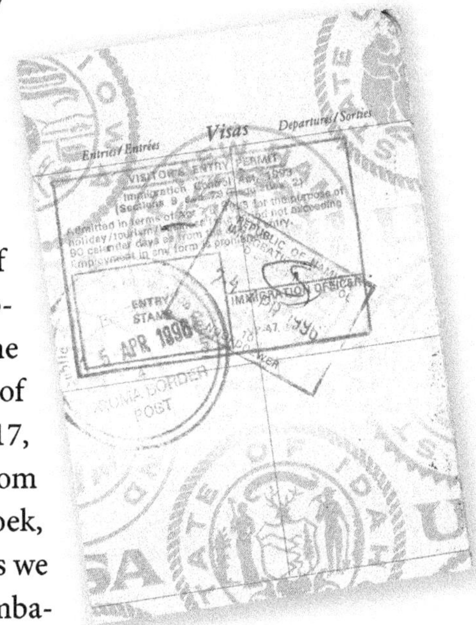

We had more than 1,500 kilometers of travel to get to our destination, but no public transport was available to suit our time schedule. Mom's entry for that final part of our trip was: "Windhoek, Namibia, April 17, 1996: Barry and I hitched rides all the way from the border of Zimbabwe to here, Windhoek, Namibia, the country's capital. From Vic Falls we took a taxi to the border . . . then from the Zimbabwe border to the Botswana border we hopped in the cab of a huge cargo truck. Then we went a short way in the back of a pick-up truck to the junction towards the Ngoma Bridge. . . . From there we caught a ride on the back of a pick-up truck with 4 black men. . . . At Ngoma we caught a ride again on the back of a pick-up with a Western couple and their 4-month-old baby. We ended up riding with Annie and Joshua and their baby all the way to Papa Falls . . . stopping off at Annie's house in the middle of the Caprivi Strip. Both Annie and her husband worked on preservation projects for the World Wildlife Fund.

"By the time we reached Papa Falls, Barry and I were starving and bought canned green beans, canned baked beans, canned sardines in tomato sauce, biscuits, cheese, 7-Up, and beer. We scarfed and played cards and looked at the spiders climbing up the ceiling of our cabin. In the morning, we walked to the dirt road and waited for a ride to the main road towards Windhoek. The first truck that came along had a freshly-slaughtered cow in the back, complete with flailing legs and hoofs. But we climbed in the back and five minutes later were on the main road. Within minutes we got a ride in the back of a truck (with a cab, thank God) with three black men that were taking school exams from Katima to Windhoek for grading. They took us all the way to Windhoek, more than 1,000km without accepting any payment. In Namibia, people greet you by clasping their palms together. The German influence is very apparent in Windhoek and in the towns along the way. . . . Clean, organized and well-landscaped. The town of Windhoek is actually aesthetically pleasing and well placed in the high desert with hills in the background. The attitude of both the blacks and whites is reserved and efficient and there seems to be quite a lot of integration as reflected in many light-skinned inhabitants."

This was Mom's last entry on the last page of her diary. She likely continued to write in a new diary, as we still were traveling for another few weeks through Namibia, South Africa, to Australia, Fiji, and then home to Sausalito. However, I could not find that other diary. The rest of the description of this trip is from my recollection.

Mom and I celebrated my hard-to-believe thirty-sixth birthday in Windhoek with a great dinner. Before continuing our journey south into Cape Town and the terminus of our Africa trip, we rented a car, which we would drive all the way down from Windhoek, Namibia, to Cape Town, South Africa, a journey of roughly 1,500 kilometers. However, we first went out to the desert at Sossusvlei in Namibia. The desert was spectacularly beautiful! I remember stopping at a store to grab some snacks and a few beers. Mom and I drove to a place where we watched the sunset over the tall sand dunes while we drank beer, ate snacks, and listened to music in the car. I don't think I have ever appreciated a sunset like that one! The vibrant colors of the sunset were like nothing I have ever seen.

We then spent the next week driving around Namibia before taking the car south to Cape Town. What a wonderful country, nice people, and very little palpable tension, unlike in other African countries, between blacks and whites.

Sussosvlei, Namibia, 1996

We loved the desert of Namibia, the colors of the sunset, the dunes, and the peacefulness. We particularly loved this cute little place we stayed in Swakopmund. The dunes rose over 1,000 feet and went right into the ocean. It was such a beautiful contrast! I remember eating in this lovely restaurant that was situated right on the beach. It was an old railway car really nicely outfitted, right on the sand.

We continued our drive south to the Fish River Canyon and stayed in a small cabin in this very small downscale "resort" right in the canyon. Mom and I decided to try our luck at fishing, but we had no equipment to fish with. We then proceeded to make our own fishing poles out of branches, using string from Mom's sewing kit for the fishing line. We carved some hooks out of an old soda can and used cheese for bait. One of my favorite books of all time comes to mind, *The Adventures of Huckleberry Finn.*

We figured we would give it a shot, not thinking we would catch any fish. We did have good "luck," however, and proceeded to catch quite a number

Table Mountain, overlooking Cape Town, South Africa, 1996

of fish. We decided to cook them on the outdoor barbecue pit at the "resort." However, after scaling and gutting the fish, we felt so bad for killing them that we could not bring ourselves to eat the meal. By that time the store was closed and what was to be our "fish-to-table" dinner ended up being some Snickers bars and a bag of potato chips we happened to have. Thankfully, we did have a few bottles of beer.

Two days later we arrived in South Africa (the southern tip at Cape Town), the last of the eight countries we traveled through during our African mega-adventure. Compared with the previous three months of travel, we were back in real civilization in Cape Town—an important city with lots of cool tourist things to do, places to eat, and a lot of backpackers, like us, to connect with.

About this time, I spoke with Marci who was pregnant with Lizzie and decided that we wanted to be back home in time for my niece Lizzie's birth. It had been a good three-plus months of travel in any case, and it was a good time to make our way back. After about four great days in Cape Town, climbing up Table Mountain, seeing the sea, visiting the wine country, and eating good food, Mom and I left Cape Town for Johannesburg and then onward. We purchased a ticket with multiple stops heading east: Fiji, then Australia, then San Francisco. We mostly hung out on the beach in Fiji and chilled. I did some diving and so did Mom, but it was not a great experience for her. We had not realized that we needed visas for Australia and arrived without them. After a long discussion with immigration authorities, they granted us twenty-four hours in Sydney. Mom and I used just about all of those twenty-four hours seeing Sydney, where I had been quite a number of times before. We finally arrived in California around mid-May 1996, just before Lizzie's birth on May 17.

The last thing in the world I had expected when Mom and I moved to London in September 1995 was to travel more than 5,000 kilometers overland down a good part of the length of that massive continent, Africa, only six months later. It was an absolutely priceless adventure that provided memories I would not trade for anything! Mom was such a trooper and a willing partner in this incredible African adventure.

It certainly was not the most rational thing to do, leaving a very good job with a good guaranteed contract for three years and a nice house setup and lifestyle in Chelsea, London, after having been on a sabbatical only one year before. Not many life partners would have counseled me to do what we did, but Mom was always ready to share these adventures with me, which is one of the many reasons why we were so perfect for each other. I know I was blessed that we found each other when we did. I was certainly taking a career risk with the decision to take a leave sabbatical from J.P. Morgan, but I followed my heart and those memories have buoyed me so much this last difficult year. They will remain with me forever. In the span of just eighteen months, from November 1994 to May 1996, Mom and I went from being good friends to being together; traveling through India, Laos, Thailand, and Burma; living in China for four months, in Sausalito for three months, and London for six months; and then for more than three months traveling from Nairobi, Kenya, to Cape Town at the tip of South Africa. Wow, what a whirlwind! However, our adventures were not finished yet.

Ashoks... they had a
some of the
beautiful
Tea ... it was
was for us the next
Sentosa Island, we
park where they had
incredible butterflies
collection (They also had an
that housed hundreds,
live ones... various
Tadpole
Cottage

8

Transition to Sausalito, then Moving to London: Round 2 (May 1996)

Mom and I arrived back in Sausalito in May of 1996, in time for both Marci's baby shower and Lizzie's birth. At that point, things with me were up in the air as to whether I would try to get another job in finance overseas or stay in the Bay Area. I was starting to feel some pressure from my responsible brain, and it entered my mind that perhaps I should get back to work. Also, we had to factor in what Mom wanted to do. I know I was so lucky that Mom was so flexible and seemed to always say yes to my plans for "next steps."

While I am sure everything worked out with our different moves, in hindsight, I do wish I had worked harder to gauge what Mom wanted and place emphasis on her priorities. In the meantime, I got a consulting job with some ex-Booz Allen consultants. They had set up their own firm, the Barents Group, which specialized in financial consulting for countries and banks in developing countries and had a lot of UN- and USAID-funded contracts. Mom was deciding whether or not to go back to the idea of nursing school. Barents Group quickly gave me assignments in both Tbilisi, Georgia (the country), and Yerevan, Armenia, and I enjoyed them both very much.

Ruzan, a student from a class I taught on financial markets in Armenia who worked for the Armenian Central Bank, recently got in touch with me after hearing about Mom's passing. She mentioned that I was in Yerevan twice, about two months before Mom and I got married and about one month after our marriage. She reminded me that on my first trip I had told many stories about Mom and Gryphen but that on the second trip all I could talk about was that I "was going to be a dad." But I am getting ahead of myself. On the second of

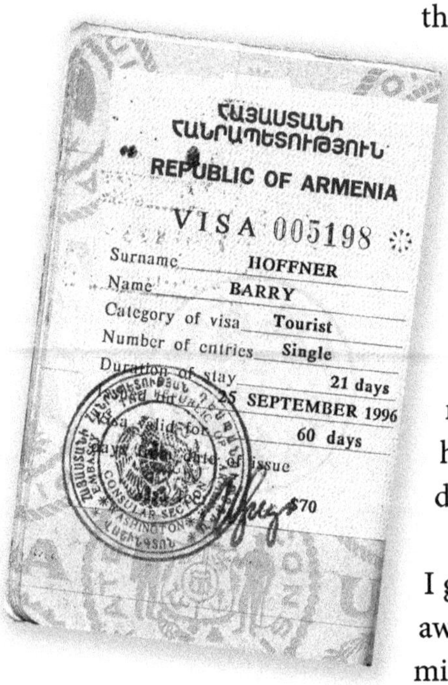

these two trips to Yerevan, a coup was attempted and the Armenian Army responded with tanks on the street.

I also had one of the more interesting nights in my life my first night in Tbilisi. On the flight from Yerevan to Tbilisi, I met a man who definitely looked like Mafia, but he seemed very intelligent and interesting as we talked. He gave me a ride from the airport to my hotel and, dropping me off, told me that he would pick me up that night at 6 p.m. for dinner.

As I was always game for a new adventure, I got in his car promptly at 6 p.m. and we drove away from the center of Tbilisi for about thirty minutes. He said we were going to a typical Georgian country restaurant. I have to admit to being a bit worried until we arrived at the place, where a long table was set with plates and plates of food and lots of alcohol. Slowly people started to arrive, all men from their late teens to senior years. I asked my new friend what the dinner was for, and he told me that it was a celebration for his son who, at eighteen years old, had just completed his first "bizness transaction." I asked what it was, and he responded that his son had purchased a Mercedes in Tbilisi (likely one stolen by Russian mobs; in those years, Moscow was the largest destination for stolen Mercedes) and driven it all the way to Kuwait (a straight-shot distance of more than 2,000 kilometers from Tbilisi) to sell it, profiting by more than $15,000. Though at that point being a parent was far from my mind (not for long), I thought that was such a cool cultural family tradition—not the part about profiting from the stolen car, rather the part about the dad's celebration of his son.

Returning home, though, I told the Barents Group that I was not willing to travel so far and be gone long periods of time in faraway places. I did love the adventure, but I also missed Mom a lot. Though she never said anything, I also felt it unfair to Mom. The pay was a lot less than what I had made at J.P.

Morgan, but I could have spent a good number of years working for Barents, traveling to off-the-beaten-path places doing real consulting work.

Barents then offered me the opportunity to do about six months of work in Mexico to help restructure the Mexican banking system that had been devastated by the 1995 Mexican peso crisis. They agreed to let me do one week in Mexico, one week off in Sausalito with Mom. I liked this idea. I could spend every other week in Sausalito doing what I wanted (with minimal work while not in-country) and the other week in Mexico City and then Guadalajara. Mom even came with me a few times to both Mexico City and Guadalajara.

I liked the intellectual discipline used in consulting, and my Barents bosses taught me a new way of breaking down a complex problem. We started with the entire problem, a completely bankrupt banking system, meaning that all Mexican banks at that point were technically bankrupt. Next, we studied data to make a few hundred hypotheses on what the problems were and how they could possibly be fixed. Then, we tested each specific hypothesis with both objective facts (data) and subjective facts (interviews with stakeholders I conducted in Spanish). It was my job to work with a local Mexican staff to analyze and test each hypothesis. In the end, Barents delivered a comprehensive report to both the Mexican government (headed by President Ernesto Zedillo) and the Central Bank that was used to put the banking system back on the road to solvency.

I very much enjoyed the six months I worked for Barents, mostly in Mexico. Working in this capacity also gave me time to figure out what I wanted to do long-term. I also greatly enjoyed my time back in Sausalito every other week. Mom and I did a lot of outdoor hiking. I remember once, while hiking up Mount Tam with Mom carrying little Gryphen, we were talking about kids and Mom seemed a bit sad. I asked her what the matter was, and she said, "I just don't know if I can have kids as I would be worried whether or not I could love them as much as I love Gryphen."

Much as I wished I could comfort Mom, I started laughing, knowing that Mom was the most caring person I ever met and, without question, that no one would ever be a more loving mother than she. Shortly thereafter, around midsummer 1996, Gryphen had two little puppies herself. Mom was absolute-

Jackie with Gryphen's puppies, 1996

ly over the moon, and her favorite thing to say was "Gryphen is such a good mother," as if it inspired her to be a good mother as well. It was obvious that with Mom's emotional intelligence and caring instinct, she did not have to be inspired to be a good mother. It was in her DNA.

Despite liking the consulting that I was doing, I knew I could not keep up that kind of off-and-on travel indefinitely and also be a good partner to Mom. Opportunities became available in the kind of work I had done for J.P. Morgan in London, with a German bank, and in Singapore, with a Japanese bank. I remember my friend from Singapore, Siu Mei, coming to visit Mom and me in Sausalito. Siu Mei was a close friend of mine when I lived in Singapore. She traveled a good part of the Silk Road in Western China with me in 1990 when we went from Beijing all the way to China's western border with Pakistan and Kyrgyzstan, a rugged three-week trip, the highlight of which was the western-most city in China, Kashgar. Kashgar was not Chinese at all then but

Jackie and Siu Mei, 1996

an amazing mix of Uighurs, Kazakhs, Hui, Kyrgyz, Tajiks, Uzbeks, and Tatars. It was the pictures I took in Kashgar, still today, one of the most interesting places I have traveled to, that Mom loved in my house in Singapore . . . and maybe even got her hooked on me? I remember passing through some small Silk Road town and stopping in a small Chinese roadside café. The owner, seeing that Siu Mei was Chinese, brought out a folded piece of paper. She unfolded it and showed it to Mei. It was a very well-drawn picture of a hamburger with all the fixings: lettuce, cheese, tomato, pickle, bun, and so on. One of the few tourists passing by had drawn it for the café owner, mentioning that if she learned to make it, she would have a lot of tourist business. So, Mei explained to her what each element of the hamburger was, even giving her the recipe for how to make catsup and mayonnaise.

Mom had met Siu Mei when we were in China, as she came to visit us in Kunming, and we all traveled together to Dali. It was the end of 1996, Siu Mei's

Gryphen in the snow, Lake Tahoe, California, 1996

birthday was on Christmas, and, of course, Mom baked her a cake. (She had a knack for endearing herself to people that way, and that was my first memory of Mom.) I remember Siu Mei saying that no one had ever actually baked her a cake before.

Right around Christmas, Siu Mei, Mom, and I drove up to Tahoe in the worst storm and traffic jam imaginable. It took us twelve hours from Sausalito to get to our house in Incline Village, and then another hour or so to dig through the snow to get to our front door. Siu Mei described the ordeal: "On this trip it was my birthday. We all went to Tahoe over Christmas—hence the horrendous traffic up there. Jackie was feeling under the weather—well now we know she was pregnant then. Coming from sunny Singapore, I was a little snow-shocked—putting on snow tires, shoveling snow (I definitely remember that!) and going for my first ski lesson. What I remember fondly was Jackie baking me a cake on my birthday (December 24) even when she wasn't feeling well."

The next day we almost lost little Gryphen frolicking around in the snowbank. After we returned home and Siu Mei headed back to Singapore, Mom and I decided to spend New Year's quietly in the town of Mendocino. It was a very memorable New Year's with Mom, maybe one of the most memorable I had with her. We had to sneak little Gryphen into the hotel because it was "no dogs allowed." I remember it raining almost all weekend long. Still we had a great time as we rang in 1997, a very memorable year for us.

Benjamin Born and Back to London, Round No. 2

In early January 1997 Mom continued to complain about not feeling so well. A store-bought pregnancy test revealed that she was pregnant. When Mom told me, I was overjoyed and excitedly asked her to marry me on the spot— but not before getting out my checkbook and asking, "How much do you want?"

Mom used to call me an "imp" because I was always joking with her about stuff, but I knew immediately it was a bad joke. I put my arms around her, asked her to marry me, and said no other news could make me happier. I still, honestly, do count that as one of the greatest days of my life. Mom and I were now committed to getting married and building our family. There is nothing better in life than being married to the love of your life and raising a family together. Mom and I decided that because she was not feeling so well, we could not go through with a big wedding at that time with all the planning that it entailed.

It was Mom's second marriage, and she really was not in the mood for a big splash. As for myself, I was generally eager to avoid bringing the kind of attention to myself that a formal wedding would entail. We were, as usual, in sync on that. Up to that point, we did not tell anyone about our plans or Mom's pregnancy. At that time Elodie, from Brazil, the younger sister of Gracie whom Baba Toba had met when she was on a trip to Egypt in 1987, was living with us in Sausalito. Every morning Mom and I would walk together, with little Gryphen, to what was then Café Soleil and have coffee. I remember once seeing Mom walking Gryphen on the Sausalito boardwalk. I then noticed that the leash appeared a bit off and realized that it was a telephone cord. I stopped to pick Mom up and asked her what the deal was with the new leash. She said, "I could not find her leash and grabbed the first thing I thought would work!" We had a neighbor, Leah, who was also a huge dog-lover, that we, particularly Mom, became close with . . . both huge dog-lovers. The owner of Café Soleil was Mom's friend Fariba. One day at the café, Mom and I came up with the idea of getting a justice of the peace to marry us in the back room of Café Soleil and having Elodie as the one "witness" we needed to make it official. We chose Valentine's Day, February 14, 1997, for the wedding day. I remember Fariba setting up a nice small table, in the backroom, where we had a bottle of champagne and some appetizers, which Gryphen kept trying to jump up and get, particularly the smoked salmon. As you both know, that café has played a large role in our family's important memories, and I feel at home there, even after all that has happened.

As part of our plan, we decided that we would announce that we were married afterward and have a nice wedding party on the San Francisco Bay two months later in April when Mom was feeling better. Mom and I informed Baba Toba, Grandpa and Grandma, Papa Dave and Grandma Shirley, and the rest of the family of our marriage after returning home from the short ceremony. Everyone was very happy for us! Grandma recalls, "I remember we got a call February 14 and Jackie on the other end said, 'Mom, are you sitting down? Barry and I were married and I'm pregnant,' all in the same breath. We were so happy for both of you!" About two months later, Mom and I went to her obstetrician and, after an ultrasound, found out that we would be having a baby boy. We were overjoyed!

Having just gotten married, with a baby on the way, also made me think a bit more about the need to get back to serious work. I felt a much stronger pull away from adventure and toward responsibility. At that point, I was still working on and off in Mexico and also in the former Soviet Union. Mom and I were trying to think of names for our soon-to-be-son and we short-listed Benjamin, Noah, Isaac, and Joseph. I remember teaching a class in Yerevan, Armenia, on financial markets and, for fun, asking the class to vote for the name they liked the best. "Benjamin" was the overwhelming favorite. I am not saying that this was the reason we chose Benjamin, as Mom and I both loved that name. Back

Barry and Jackie on their wedding day, Sausalito, California, 1997

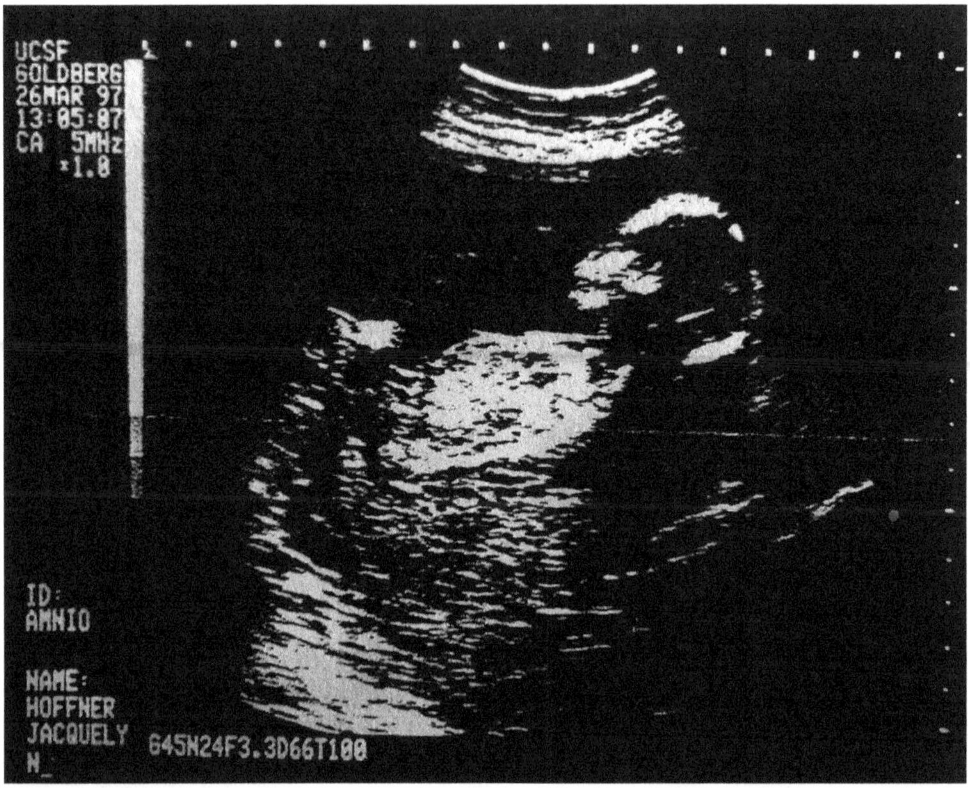

An ultrasound of Benjamin, March 1997

home in Sausalito, Aunt Marci and Uncle Brian threw Mom a really nice baby shower at their house, which Grandpa, Grandma, and Baba Toba drove up for. Even while pregnant, early on, Mom took a couple of trips with me to Guadalajara where I was working every other week. It was so nice to have her with me on those trips. As the Mexican real-estate market was sharply lower than it was in previous years, Mom and I came close to buying a house in Guadalajara, right on a nice lake with money I had made investing in the Russian stock market.

When back in Sausalito, I started thinking about a more permanent, stable job. We really liked the idea of staying in the Bay Area or at least in California, but I also knew that my greatest earning potential was overseas. I looked at

A Baby Shower for Barry and Jackie Hoffner
Sunday, August 17th
4:00-6:00 p.m.
at the home of
Brian and Marci Dragun
2608 Prindle Road
Belmont, CA
RSVP by August 10th to Marci at (415) 631-9098
Baby Hoffner is registered at Lullaby Lane (San Bruno), Toys R Us and Target.
!Nursery is decorated in bright colors!

Baby shower for Jackie, Belmont, California, 1997

a couple of job opportunities in the Bay Area. One was working for the San Francisco Federal Reserve Bank, focusing on the Asian markets and banking system. It certainly would have been an interesting job, though the pay was less than what I was used to.

Finally, I decided that I could not work well in a bureaucratic government job after the kinds of jobs I had before and thus declined the offer. Another interesting opportunity, which Mom went with me to interview for as a finalist, was with an equity fund manager in La Jolla, near San Diego, focusing on emerging markets. In the end, I did not get that job. I did, however, have two job offers with large banks, one with Swiss Bank Corp in London, focusing on emerging markets in Eastern Europe, and the other with Nomura Securities in

Diane, Jackie, and Lyell at, wedding party, April 1997

Singapore.

Mom and I talked it over and decided on London. She knew that my heart was set on delving further into the newly developing financial markets in Eastern Europe, particularly in Russia. We also thought that London would be the best environment for Mom and little Benjamin.

In April, we rented out a boat that cruised the San Francisco Bay for our wedding party. All the grandparents, aunts, uncles, nephews, and nieces were in attendance. It was a really nice, fun day out on the bay topped off by some wonderful music by our friend Noelle Hampton.

After I accepted the job with Swiss Bank Corp in London, I finished up my last consulting assignments overseas in late May 1997, and we started preparing for Benjamin's birth. At that point, Mom was feeling very healthy. We also had

Jackie and Barry, wedding party, April 1997

made our first close friends, Heidi and Greg, whom we met in a birth class at the Left Bank restaurant in Larkspur. Heidi described our fortuitous meeting: "There were between 10–15 couples who attended this class and all through the class Barry threw in humorous remarks about the vivid descriptions made by the nurse of, for example, the uterus, the placenta, etc. Greg and I were intrigued by his sense of humor, and during the break we introduced ourselves and were instantly taken by this beautiful couple, their friendly and intelligent demeanor. To our astonishment, we realized that the wives had the same due date, 9/9/97 . . . what a date!" Other than family, Heidi was one of Mom's few (current) female friends to actually see her pregnant. Heidi talked about Mom while she was pregnant with Benjamin: "One day we decided to spend the day at Stinson Beach. Jackie brought Gryphen and together we both showed off our

Jackie and Heidi, Stinson Beach, California, 1997

huge bellies walking down the beach. She was such a beauty and tiny, so much smaller and shorter than myself. We were so proud to say that we had the same due date!"

Shortly thereafter—I remember the day like it was yesterday—Heidi, Greg, Mom, and I were having dinner at our house in Sausalito at 303 South Street, where we were living with Elodie, when Mom said that she was starting to

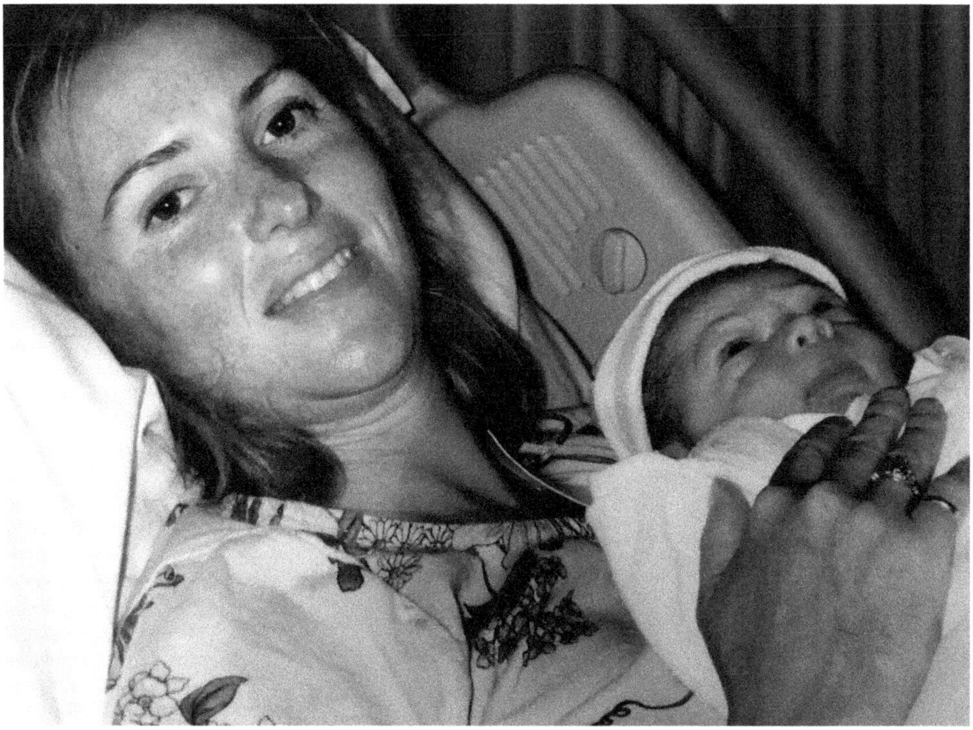

Jackie and Benjamin, September 9, 1997

feel weird. I quickly got her stuff together and we were off to Marin General Hospital. After something like fifteen hours, Benjamin was born. Again, Heidi was the only family or friend to see Jackie in labor. She described the events: "I decided to pay Jackie a visit and was led by a nurse to her hospital room. There I found Barry very much engaged with the Monday night football game playing on the hospital TV. Jackie was sitting at the edge of her bed suffering through waves of painful contractions. Barry eagerly explained to me that the IV in Jackie was a 'drip of potassium.' Jackie, being the scientist, hissed at him, correcting him instantly with "It's Pitocin not potassium." We have joked and laughed about that for the next two decades!" And voilà, Benjamin was born!

Benjamin, I explained what your birth meant to me in a letter to you a few years ago on your birthday: "Dear Benjamin, shortly before Mom got pregnant, I was going through a bit of a difficult time . . . I had achieved a good bit in my career, made some money, been a lot of places, but I strongly felt something was missing . . . I was questioning the meaning of life. Not from the point of being severely depressed . . . but something was clearly not right with me.

"All of that changed the day Mom told me she was pregnant with you. It is hard to explain and probably hard for you to understand, but it was almost like seeing life completely differently, an important reason for being alive and wanting to be the best I could be for the sake of my new child and for the love of my life, Mom. That day changed everything for Mom and me."

I can't explain the feeling we had—there are no words except a feeling of power, ecstasy, like *everything* is right in the world, like it was the beginning of our lives as well. I have no doubt that on that day I witnessed my first miracle! I was fortunate to have had that feeling twice in my life, on the days that both of you were born. I hope you two know that special feeling one day. *There is nothing like it!* I remember Mom and me getting back to our home in Sausalito on the third night and you, Benjamin, sleeping through everything to the point that we called the nurse at the hospital concerned that you were sleeping too much. The nurse joked that we were lucky and that it was a good problem to have! I remember Mom and me kind of looking at each other saying, "I can't believe they actually let us take home a real, live baby!"

Right around that time, Princess Diana was killed in a vehicle accident, only steps from where I lived in Paris in 1987 at Place de l'Alma. It was a very emotional time. Mom and I had a serious discussion about how we were going to raise Benjamin, and Mom willingly volunteered that she would be happy to raise Benjamin Jewish but had some questions for a rabbi. We went to Tiburon to meet with Rabbi Lavey Derby. Mom asked some excellent questions and particularly liked how the rabbi answered her question about what Jesus meant to the Jews. She also became comfortable with the covenant of the Jewish people to circumcise boys when they are born. Thus, seven days later we followed the ancient Jewish tradition and had Benjamin's bris at our house with both Papa Dave and Grandpa Lyell sharing the joint honorary role with us.

I remember taking Benjamin in a stroller just about every morning to Café Soleil to have my coffee, read the newspaper, and marvel at little Benjamin, while Mom got to sleep in. Those were very special days; our hearts were so

Grandpa Lyell and Papa Dave at Benjamin's bris, Sausalito, California, 1997

full! Mom and I also took trips to Las Vegas and Los Angeles to visit Baba Toba, Papa Dave, and Grandma Shirley and to Orange County to see Grandma and Grandpa.

About six weeks later, I was off to New York for training with my new company, Swiss Bank Corp, while Mom took Benjamin to Iowa to spend time with Grandma and Grandpa. It was crazy how Mom and I would move on a dime, from China to Sausalito, from Sausalito to London, from Africa back to Sausalito, and then from Sausalito back to London, again, all in the span of a bit more than two years. Mom joined me in New York with little Benjamin, only three months old, for about three weeks. Mom and I bought tickets for a classical concert and took Benjamin—what were we thinking?

While training in New York, I got the news that Swiss Bank Corp had announced a merger with UBS (another large Swiss bank). I was 2-for-2. That is, in my last two jobs, both Chemical Bank and Swiss Bank Corp announced mergers within the first week of my joining them. As the old saying goes, "We plan, and God laughs!"

This time, no matter what, with responsibility not just for myself but also for Mom and Benjamin, I was determined to stick with the job until the end. Around mid-December, Mom and I moved, with little Benjamin, to London and stayed in a service apartment until we could find a place to live. As our stuff was on the way to London, we did not have much with us. I remember Mom giving Benjamin a bath in the sink of our service flat in London. Mom and I decided to spend Christmas in Paris and took Benjamin on the train from London to Paris to stay in my favorite place, Île Saint-Louis.

Benjamin was only a little more than three months old. I remember Christmas Eve being a cold, rainy evening. Mom and I pushed Benjamin in a stroller, trying to find a restaurant that would let us in with a baby. Finally, we found one restaurant on the main street, and we had a nice Christmas dinner. On every trip back to Paris, although the restaurant changed owners many times, we always remembered that place!

A few weeks later, Mom found us the most wonderful, adorable little house with the name Tadpole Cottage at 57 Highgate West Hill in the little village of Highgate. Everything about it was perfect! What a special time in our lives. We lived just off the main square, near a nice park. Mom and I would often walk with Benjamin across a huge park, Hampstead Heath, to the village of Hampstead, go to the Spaniards Inn for a beer or hang out at Kenwood Gardens, and take a stroll to the nearby cemetery in Highgate, where none other than Karl Marx is interred.

I commuted to work via bus. Shortly after I started work, I learned that because of the merger, most of our business was being shut down until the merger was finished, which would take about three or four months. Although this did create some additional uncertainty, it gave me extra time to be with Mom and Benjamin. I also used that time to start learning Russian, using the Pimsleur tapes. I began playing a lot of chess with my Russian friend and colleague Pavel, from whom I was learning a great deal about Russia. As Mom always did, she made some nice friends right away—Cynthia, Rika (from Fin-

Tadpole Cottage, Highgate, London, 1997

land) from whom we would eventually get Muffin, and Katherine (also from Finland), who would be the one, a little over a year later, to take Mom to the hospital when Daniel was born. Mom and I also used the opportunity to travel some weekends with Benjamin, although he was not even six months old. We went to Dublin one weekend. We took a memorable trip to Israel, Mom and Benjamin's first of a number of trips to the country. We went to Venice another weekend to see some of our Italian friends we had met in China, principally Matteo. Benjamin, you got very sick on this trip from all the cigarette smoking at the party that Matteo organized, in his apartment, in our honor. Mom and I really questioned going on that getaway. Perhaps, we were always too game for a new mini-adventure, even with a little one. This was surely my fault! We also traveled around Scotland on another weekend. Mom had two part-time

Benjamin and Jackie, Jerusalem, Israel, 1998

babysitters helping her, both of whom we liked a lot, Janna from the Czech Republic and Orly from France. We had visits from Grandma and Grandpa, Baba Toba, Heidi and Greg, and cousin Trevor's mom, Aunt Jenn.

One very funny, typically Mom, story occurred while Grandpa and Grandma were in London visiting us. At that time Gryphen was living with Grandpa and Grandma. Thus when they came to London, Mom arranged for Gryphen to go from Orange County, where Grandpa and Grandma lived to Heidi and Greg in Marin, who kindly agreed to watch her. Unfortunately, I cannot remember

Barry and Benjamin, Israel, 1998

how she got up north. As Grandpa and Grandma were literally on a plane returning to Orange County from London, Jackie spoke with Heidi and realized that Gryphen has been misbehaving, peeing, pooping in their house and not eating very much. Although parts of this story are a bit fuzzy, Mom, from London, somehow arranged to have a driver pick Gryphen up at Heidi and Greg's house and take her to San Francisco International Airport and check her in to fly back to Orange County with the timing to match Grandpa and Grandma's return flight from London. Well, somehow Gryphen's papers were not in order and she was not allowed to fly, so the driver promptly took Gryphen back to Heidi and Greg's. Mom frantically called Grandpa, who had just returned from London, and asked if he would drive up from Orange County to Marin County and get Gryphen. Grandpa arrived at Heidi and Greg's, quickly said hello, picked Gryphen up and drove her back to Orange County . . . a roundtrip of close to sixteen hours. As Grandpa said, "I loved to do things for Jackie because she was always so appreciative!" There have never been two more helpful grandparents than Grandpa and Grandma. One of the very best things about Mom, as you guys both know, is that there was never a dull moment.

As we got into the summer, and the merger progressed between Swiss Bank Corp and UBS, a number of my colleagues were getting fired. This time, I was not on a guaranteed contract and, again, was determined to move my career forward. Unlike my fired colleagues, I was lucky. I was offered the opportunity to move to Moscow and run the Russian trading business for the new UBS.

Shortly thereafter, one of my colleagues had moved to ING-Barings, which was looking for someone to go to Moscow to run its Russian trading business. I also had an offer to join a large UK bank, with ex-colleagues Pablo and Pavel, and stay in London. Around that time, the then-president of Russia, Boris Yeltsin, arguably one of world history's most important figures of the 1990s, increasingly appeared to be coming unhinged. He was regularly caught on camera totally drunk and was firing prime ministers every few months (he actually went through five different prime ministers in the span of just one year: Chernomyrdin, Kiriyenko, Primakov, Stepashin, and finally Putin). The Communists appeared to be gaining traction politically once again. Russia was taking on too much debt which started to look increasingly financially unsustainable.

Still, I was fascinated by Russia and had already devoted a good amount of time to learning Russian. Thus, I took a trip to Moscow to look at both Russian opportunities. Clearly the ING-Barings opportunity was much better, because ING had a big presence all across Eastern Europe with a big Moscow office while UBS had a quite a small office.

Before I could proceed any further, I needed to have a serious discussion with Mom about moving to Moscow or staying in London. Previously, I really did not want to run the risk of stressing Mom out until I had some firm offers.

I was lucky to have three solid job opportunities, but my heart was really in going to Russia. I remember taking Mom on a trip to Saint Petersburg for a weekend in early summer so she could see a bit of Russia before we made our minds up. Funny enough, though, I don't think we brought Benjamin with us. We may have left him with our babysitters, Orly and Janna, which is hard to believe given how young he was. We had such an amazing weekend, going to the Hermitage Museum and walking all around the city until 11 p.m. as it was still light out. Saint Petersburg was so interesting. On the way home, without me even having to ask, Mom turned to me and said, "Let's move to Russia!" That was what I had wanted to do all along and was hoping that Mom would want to. That she came out and said it gave me great comfort.

I would not trade the four years of raising our family in Moscow, Russia, for anything in the world. What a tremendous experience it was in so many ways, and I thank Mom for allowing it to happen. It was an absolutely unique opportunity, in a country rich with history, going through a historic transition. Moreover, I had a "solid" job with a good company. We decided together that I would accept the offer from ING-Barings. It was June 1998 at that point and we were to move to Moscow in August, though I would start traveling there right away while Mom went back to California with Benjamin. I remember having dinner one night with one of my ex-colleagues and he asked me if I wanted to have more kids. I said, "For sure, though right now we are in the middle of a move to Russia and with Benjamin less than twelve months old, we should probably wait a bit." Honest to God, Mom called me that night from California from the US to tell me that she had just learned that she was pregnant with Daniel. I could not have been happier! I called up a few colleagues the next day and we went to a pub in Hampstead to celebrate the unexpected new child on the way!

9

The Big Russian Adventure (starting August 1998)

I remember during the summer of 1998 watching the World Cup games in London, in pubs around Highgate and Hampstead. Mom and Benjamin were back in California and Iowa, preparing for our move to Moscow and seeing family. Russia was experiencing serious financial and political turmoil. Right as we were about to move to Moscow, the Russian government announced that it was defaulting on its sovereign local debt, a major blow in the financial markets. The Russian ruble quickly lost more than 90% of its value, going from three rubles to one USD to 30 rubles to one USD.

Imagine, literally from one day to the next, the real value of your life savings decreasing by 90%! That is what happened in Russia on August 13, 1998. It was chaos in Moscow. I had lived through hyperinflation in Argentina in 1985, when inflation was roughly at 500%. The ticket price for the bus ride I took to work in Buenos Aires increased from the morning trip to the afternoon return trip and then again the next morning. That's why, in Moscow, I asked Mom to stock up on a number of important, hard-to-find items, principally diapers, baby food, and so on.

It was also chaos in Western financial markets despite the fact that the Russian financial markets were relatively tiny in size compared with other global markets. In the ten days following Russia's default, the US stock market lost more than 10% of its value. Some Western financial institutions were very exposed to the Russian financial markets.

One in particular, the hedge fund Long-Term Capital, run supposedly by some of the greatest financial minds in the world, was taken over by the US Federal Reserve and wound down. To give you an idea, the Russian stock market lost 98.5% of its value in less than one year from 1997 to '98. Russian banks started closing down. Unbelievably, Russia's largest eurobond (denominated in US dollars) with a coupon of 12¾% and a 25-year maturity traded as low as 25 cents on the dollar. Russia had yet to default on its eurobonds and ended up never having to. Trading as low as 25 cents on the dollar, you would get all your money back for only two years of coupons and still own the principal and future coupon payments. This turned out to be a tremendous investment opportunity!

The market was signaling that Russia, as we knew it, was finished and the Communists were coming back to power. In fact, the Communist Party really was gaining power and marching in the streets. It was, to say the least, an interesting, but challenging and uncertain, time to be in Russia.

At that point, Benjamin's first birthday, we were staying in the Metropol Hotel in downtown Moscow and had started looking for apartments. We found a nice apartment in central Moscow. I still remember the name of the street, Znamenka. Next on our list was to find a babysitter to help out with Benjamin. We, no doubt, lucked out finding the best nanny one could ever find, Valentina Kornieva, who, as you know, continues to be like family to us today.

Owing to the economic crisis, many foreigners were being sent home by their companies as they closed or slimmed down their businesses. One Brazilian couple I met were leaving and gave me Valentina's name and number. In those early days in Moscow, I spoke a little Russian from listening to Pimsleur tapes, but Mom spoke no Russian. Yet I remember the first night Mom and I went out to dinner and returned home. Valentina launched into a long commentary on Benjamin in Russian (Valentina spoke very little English). From the few words I could pick up, I could tell that she was already in love with him.

After a few more times out we could see that Valentina really did love Benjamin deeply and also how much Benjamin loved her. Though we were, at that point, looking only for a babysitter from time to time, Mom and I discussed the idea of hiring Valentina as Benjamin's full-time nanny, even though Mom was around the apartment a lot. She could help with the cooking and cleaning and with Benjamin and also keep Mom company. We all genuinely loved Valentina. Also, Mom was pregnant with Daniel during the winter in Moscow, and it

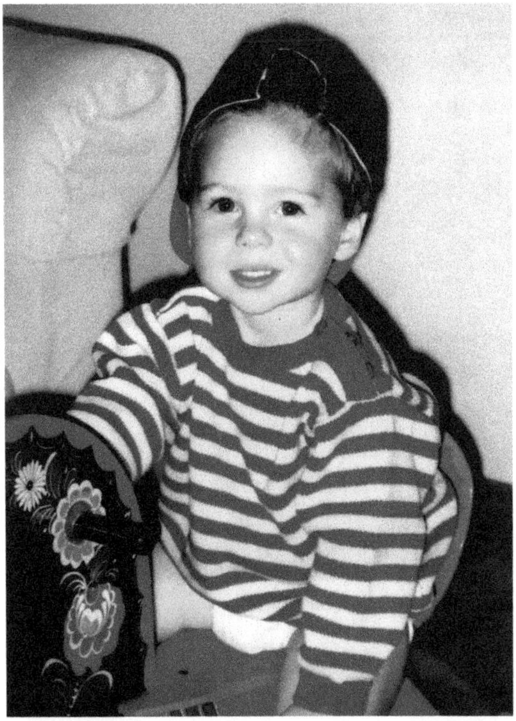

◂ Benjamin in the Moscow apartment, Znamenka Street, Moscow, Russia, 1998

▾ Daniel, Valentina and Benjamin, Moscow River, Serebryany Bor, Moscow, 2001

was not always easy to get around. Valentina quickly became part of the family as did her two children. Mom would eventually learn a good bit of Russian, but as she liked to say, without any command of Russian grammar, "What's the point?" I used to think that Mom and Valentina had somehow developed their own grammar-less subdialect of the language, sprinkling in some English words and using hand gestures when needed.

As mom's friend Suzanne said, "Your mother's Russian was excellent; better than mine ever was, and I stayed there for sixteen years. If she couldn't communicate with words, she was excellent at miming, or she would just use pure hope that whomever she was communicating with understood her. And if they didn't understand, it would usually become a humorous story." (Like when our driver Kiril came back with twelve times the number of toilet paper rolls that Mom had wanted.) Suzanne continued, "Your Mom had a great quality in being able to laugh at herself. One of the many reasons why she was loved by so many." Mom and I were really liking our life in Moscow, though it wasn't always easy. We found everything and everyone so interesting! We started to make some close friends, like Zora, a Ukrainian-American, and Franck, a Moroccan Jew who grew up in France and Spain. Zora often told the story about how she met Mom after they both had arrived in Moscow around the same time: "It was 1998, right after the crisis hit Russia when Franck and I moved to Moscow with four-month-old Markian. The first thing I knew I had to do was join the International Women's Club to find friends, learn where to buy diapers, how to hire a nanny and find a baby group. I arrived first thing in the morning to the first IWC event in the center of town wearing a T-shirt and jeans with baby in tow. At the entrance, I nearly got rejected for not having the proper attire and bringing a baby. I was reminded that it was clear that children were not allowed to this event. Upon entering the elegantly furnished building (which was some kind of former palace) in my scruffy jeans, tattered hair, bloodshot eyes from too little sleep, and T-shirt with baby spit on it, it was clear that I did not belong here. And then I saw Jackie, like a ray of sunshine bursting through the clouds, across a crowded room of elegantly dressed women. She was in the same condition and attire as me, but with the addition of a huge chocolate stain across her white T-shirt. It was clear that we both didn't belong to this crowd but were cut from the same cloth and had the same mission. It must have been destiny. We clicked right away and I knew at that moment I had met my best friend for life."

We also had Valentina, which meant that Benjamin received very good care from us three. Because the Russian market was so disengaged, at that point, from Western financial markets, I was home practically every evening by 6.

I was not even 100% sure that we would be able to stay in Moscow because so many foreign banks were transferring their expensive expat staff out of Russia given the financial collapse. I spent a good deal of time putting a plan together for ING-Barings senior management to demonstrate business opportunities in Russia. I had envisioned, for ING-Barings, good business opportunities if they remained with close-to-full staff in Russia in the financial markets department, despite the financial collapse, particularly with so much of the competition leaving.

The presentation went over well, and they rewarded me with a three-year guaranteed contract to stay in Moscow and continue to build their financial markets businesses, thus cementing our plans for the following three years. That was a huge relief. As I look back, that contract ensured that our family would have the most consequential four years of our lives together.

My first week at work, the head of security of ING-Barings told me that I needed to get a local driving permit and took me to the equivalent of the DMV in Moscow. We went into the office of the head of the place, and the security spoke with the guy there in very fast Russian, which I had trouble following. He then told me that I would need to sit in front of a computer and take a driver's test to get my license. I sat at the computer and, to my surprise, saw a number of questions, all in Russian. My Russian was not yet up to speed to be able to successfully take the test. I asked the ING person, "What should I do, everything is in Russian?" He responded, "Barry, just press the button for any answer. It doesn't really matter."

Thus, I followed instructions. After the test, we went back in the office and the ING person handed my passport to the man at the desk, together with 3,000 rubles (roughly $100). The person at the desk held out his hand and said, "Pozdravlayu, Gospodin Xhoffner, vi zdali ekzamen" (Congratulations, Mr. Hoffner, you passed the exam). I used to drive myself to work every day, early in the morning. Kiril, our driver, would pick up the car at ING Bank, go run errands for Mom, or take Mom and you boys where you needed to go, and then drop the car off for me in the afternoon to return home.

On one of the first few days of driving, I got stopped by the police. My Russian was not good, and they were not nice. Even trying to play dumb, I knew that I would not get out of it without giving them some money. From then on, I got stopped at least a few times per week. After the first few months, when they stopped me, I did not even acknowledge them. I simply folded up a 100-ruble note (roughly $3) in a piece of paper, cracked the window slightly, and held it out for them to take without even looking at them. I called this "the Moscow road tax."

Mom was happy to have a good doctor in Russia, an Englishwoman named Dr. Bascum, who, on one visit to check on her pregnancy, informed us that we would be having a boy. We were thrilled! As we got through the winter, it was time to start planning for Mom to go to London where we wanted Daniel to be born. (We had already decided that Daniel would be his name.) We rented an apartment in Hampstead, which we loved (just across the Heath from Highgate where we had lived before), and Mom moved there two months before Daniel was born. Initially Mom went to London for about two weeks by herself to look for a place and left Benjamin with Valentina and me. Another week, Julie came to visit Mom in London, to celebrate her 40th birthday, while Valentina was there, and they all went to Paris as well with little Benjamin.

One weekend, with Mom in London and Benjamin and me together in Moscow, I decided on a whim, during a four-day weekend, to take a train from Moscow to Vilnius, Lithuania, with Benjamin. We booked our own sleeping car. Benjamin was great, and we had a lot of fun on the train and also in Vilnius. Benjamin was such a good traveler! I loved the idea of being able to continue living an adventurous life, though a little scaled back.

While Mom was in London, we decided to move farther out of the center of Moscow where the air was cleaner and where there was more green space. During that time, I started searching for houses and found a lovely little house in an area called Serebryany Bor (Silvery Woods). It is from this experience that we used the name for two of our properties in Cloverdale: Silverwood

Our house in Serebryany Bor, Moscow, 1999

Ranch and the Silverwood Building in downtown Cloverdale. The image and memories from our place in Serebryany Bor will always carry a lot of meaning in my life!

At that point, Mom was within about six weeks of giving birth to Daniel and could not travel. In those days, there was also no such thing as taking pictures with an iPhone and sending them to Mom in London so that she could see the small two-floor house I found in Serebryany Bor. I described it to her. It is true that, by that point, I had fallen in love with the house despite its quirkiness: an old blue wooden house set in a compound with three other houses on an island where the nature was as nice as it gets in Moscow. Just beyond our front door was a gate that led immediately to the Moscow River, where in the winter people would cross-country ski and ice-fish and in the summer boat and swim. It was a really nice setting! After speaking with Mom, I secured the house and had all of our things moved from the apartment. As I think back about that

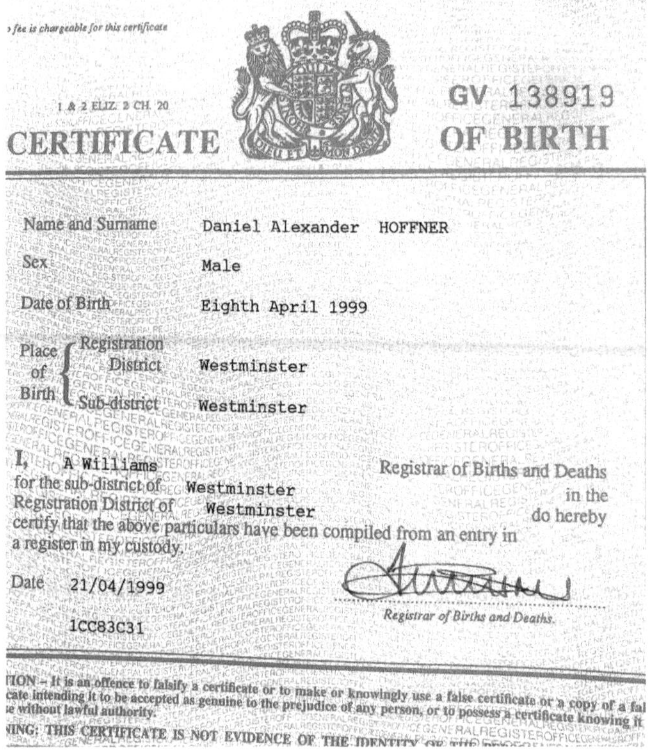

fee is chargeable for this certificate

1 & 2 ELIZ. 2 CH. 20

GV 138919

CERTIFICATE OF BIRTH

Name and Surname Daniel Alexander HOFFNER

Sex Male

Date of Birth Eighth April 1999

Place of Birth { Registration District Westminster
Sub-district Westminster

I, A Williams Registrar of Births and Deaths for the sub-district of Westminster in the Registration District of Westminster do hereby certify that the above particulars have been compiled from an entry in a register in my custody.

Date 21/04/1999

1CC83C31

Registrar of Births and Deaths.

TION – It is an offence to falsify a certificate or to make or knowingly use a false certificate or a copy of a fal cate intending it to be accepted as genuine to the prejudice of any person, or to possess a certificate knowing it e without lawful authority.

NING: THIS CERTIFICATE IS NOT EVIDENCE OF THE IDENTITY OF THE PERSON

Daniel's birth certificate, Westminster, London, 1999

house, a smile comes to my face. That house was about as cute, quaint, cozy, rustic, and full of character as it gets and, on top of it, we started and raised our family there!

Mom and I had planned for me to take two weeks off work starting one week before Daniel's due date, which was supposed to be roughly around my birthday, on April 16, 1999. We figured I would be there one week before Daniel's birth and stay for Daniel's first week. Mom would then move back to Moscow when it was OK to do so, roughly four to six weeks after Daniel was born. Sure enough, Daniel came early to change these plans. That day would still rank as one of the strangest but best feelings I have ever had.

I got a call, from Grandma, very early in my morning of April 8, 1999 (it was even earlier in London). Grandma had traveled to London to be with Mom and help out a month or so before Daniel's birth. Grandma said that Mom had

Lindfield Gardens, Hampstead, London, 1999

gone into labor very early in the morning, that Mom's Finnish friend Katherine had picked her up and taken her to Portland Hospital, and that in less than one hour Mom had given birth to Daniel. Katherine later described the events to me: "We lived literally right next to each other in London on Lindfield Gardens. You were in Moscow and Jackie was with her mother and Benjamin, and we saw each other all the time. The due date was getting closer, and you were arriving in just a couple days but as things would turn out Daniel was in a hurry to get out, and so one night around 4 a.m. our phone rings and it's Jackie telling me 'Katherine, it's time.' I grab the keys of the little Ford Fiesta that we had and run out to the car in order to move it in front of your house. Kari's motorbike, the very one, was parked right behind the Fiesta and in my rush of course I bumped into it and it fell over (it got a small dent which we always fondly referred to as the Jackie and Daniel dent). Literally three minutes after four I was in your apartment where your mother was making sure that Jackie had all she needed packed for me to take. Sweet little Benjamin was sound asleep. Jackie was extraordinarily calm and happy. She was calming us down and reassuring everyone that everything was fine. The contractions were getting so close to each other, we had to stop on our way to the car several times. Finally, in the car I frantically tried to think of the shortest way to Portland Hospital, and although it was perhaps the shortest it must have had a record number of speed bumps for such a short distance.

"I vividly remember Jackie looking at me, 'Seriously?!' The streets were empty, and finally we make it to Portland Hospital and I just leave the car on Great Portland Street right after a bus stop next to the hospital. Jackie is almost running inside, and me with the bag right behind her. As they show her into her room, they ask me who I am and if I am staying, and since we had not had any opportunity to even contemplate this kind of situation with Jackie, I had no idea what she wanted. So I stay to make sure she is settled and taken care of, and then ask her if she wants me to stay or wait outside. She is in full labor by now, and with a crazed birth-giving look she hisses at me 'Katherine, I do not care!' I almost start laughing and decide that if it were me I would not want to be with strangers only, that I would want to have the chance to share this moment with her, you, Daniel, and Benjamin one day.

"So I stayed with her and tried to say the right things, encouraging her. And once again she demonstrated her incredible strength, fun and cool character and zest for life by giving me another one of her deep blue-eyed looks and hissed at me once more 'I KNOW it's going to be OK!' Daniel was born in a blink of an eye. Jackie was incredible. So positive, matter of fact, so strong, oozing serenity and so happy. Happy. And beautiful little Daniel was like an extension of her as she held him. I got to hold him too. I was so grateful to have been there. You probably did not know, but Kari and I had wanted children for many years without success. Nothing was wrong, we were just not lucky yet then. They say that when a woman is present at another woman's childbirth she is exposed to incredible amounts of hormones. That something is triggered . . . I was pregnant with Rodion soon after. I feel so blessed to have had this connection with Jackie."

I spoke with Mom and was assured she and little Daniel were okay. The next roughly fifteen to eighteen hours proved to be the most impatient hours I had ever spent in my life. The only flight out of Moscow that day was in the evening, and by the time I reached London and went directly to Portland Hospital, it was midnight. Thus, I did not see Daniel until April 9, 1999, even though his birthdate was April 8. As a result, my favorite number became 9, because Benjamin was born on September 9, that is, the 9th month and the 9th day, and the first time I got to hold Daniel was April 9, 1999, or the 99th day in 1999. I have to say that I felt like a caged animal for the fifteen to eighteen hours between the time I found out that Daniel had come into this world and the time I got to see him and Mom. I had a son in the world that I had not yet seen. Even if it lasted for only a bit more than half a day, it was a very strange feeling. I did not know what to do with myself. I had so much bottled-up energy and could not focus on work at all.

Finally, I got to London and got to hold Daniel. Back in our apartment, Mom gave him the nickname Winston Churchill, one of Mom's favorite historical characters. She thought baby Daniel kind of looked like him. We had the Jewish mohel come and perform an abbreviated bris. In the beginning, it was hard for Mom to give Daniel the attention he deserved and at the same time be with Benjamin, still a baby himself and taking the new scene in. Daniel was one of the few babies to have his own passport at the age of two weeks.

Right around that time, I turned thirty-nine years old, and Mom wrote me a typically sweet birthday card that read: "Dearest Barry, I know this birthday of yours is overshadowed by the recent birth of Daniel, but I think you're probably happy that the focus is off you and on baby Daniel's bris. However, for your 39th birthday, I want you to know that I'm thinking of you and hoping that we will celebrate this day for <u>you</u> just a little. I wish for this birthday that you have many, many years of abundant happiness and memories with your two sons . . . and any other children that may enter your life . . . and with me. We all love you so much and I hope you realize from time to time how special you are to me. Love, Jackie."

We decided that it might be a good idea for me to take Benjamin away for a few days, and so the next day Benjamin and I hopped on a train to Paris for

Daniel's first days at our flat at Lindfield Gardens, 1999

three days. We, of course, stayed at our favorite place on Île Saint-Louis. It was during this trip that little Benjamin and I spent time with Noelle Hampton and her family who were visiting Paris. By coincidence, they were staying in an apartment on Île Saint-Louis.

Noelle played the guitar at our wedding party on the boat.

After about four weeks, it was time for Grandma to return to California and for Mom and Daniel to come to Moscow. I was excited to take Mom to our new house in Serebryany Bor. We pulled into the compound and up to the front door. Mom asked me to hold Daniel and stay with Benjamin in the car while she looked inside the house first. Mom came out after about five minutes in tears, and I asked, "Are those tears of happiness or displeasure?" to which Mom replied, "I know I will grow to love the house!" The house was definitely quirky, and Mom had expectations of a more modern house, but she grew to

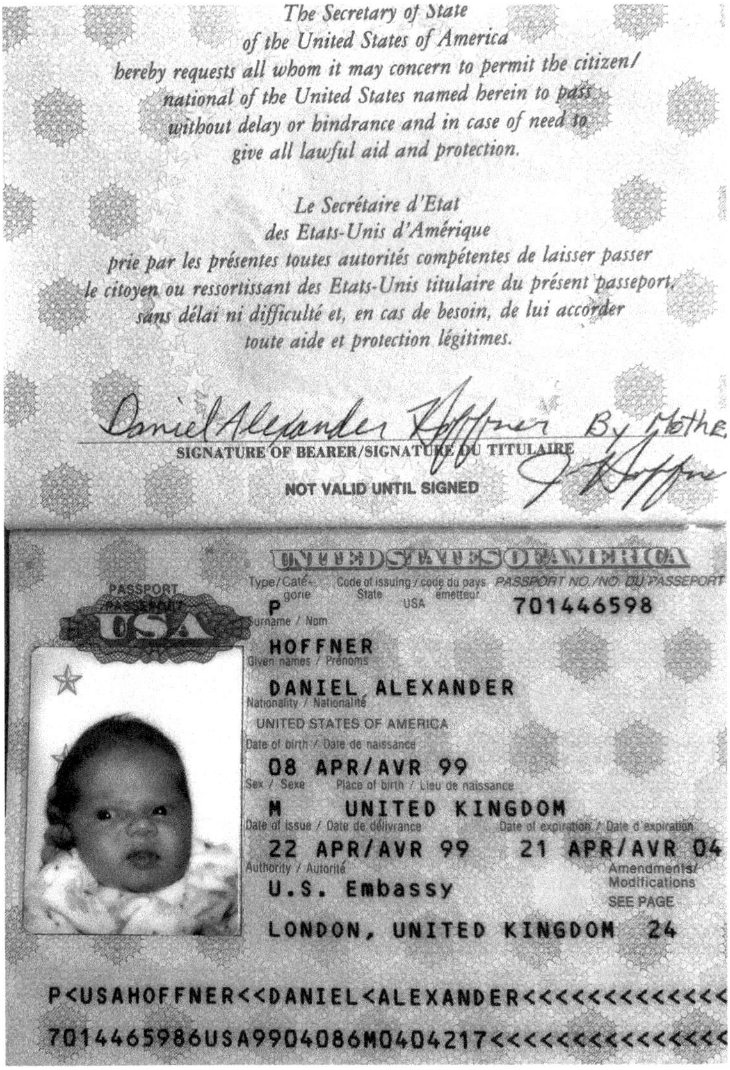
The Secretary of State
of the United States of America
hereby requests all whom it may concern to permit the citizen/
national of the United States named herein to pass
without delay or hindrance and in case of need to
give all lawful aid and protection.

Le Secrétaire d'Etat
des Etats-Unis d'Amérique
prie par les présentes toutes autorités compétentes de laisser passer
le citoyen ou ressortissant des Etats-Unis titulaire du présent passeport,
sans délai ni difficulté et, en cas de besoin, de lui accorder
toute aide et protection légitimes.

SIGNATURE OF BEARER/SIGNATURE DU TITULAIRE

NOT VALID UNTIL SIGNED

UNITED STATES OF AMERICA

PASSPORT / PASSEPORT USA

Type/Catégorie: P
Code of issuing State / code du pays émetteur: USA
PASSPORT NO./NO. DU PASSEPORT: 701446598
Surname / Nom: HOFFNER
Given names / Prénoms: DANIEL ALEXANDER
Nationality / Nationalité: UNITED STATES OF AMERICA
Date of birth / Date de naissance: 08 APR/AVR 99
Sex / Sexe: M
Place of birth / Lieu de naissance: UNITED KINGDOM
Date of issue / Date de délivrance: 22 APR/AVR 99
Date of expiration / Date d'expiration: 21 APR/AVR 04
Authority / Autorité: U.S. Embassy LONDON, UNITED KINGDOM 24
Amendments/Modifications: SEE PAGE

P<USAHOFFNER<<DANIEL<ALEXANDER<<<<<<<<<<<<<<
7014465986USA9904086M0404217<<<<<<<<<<<<<<<<

Daniel's first passport, 1999

love that house, even more than the rest of us! Even today, thinking about that house and the memories we created inside it, as we were evolving as a family, brings me great comfort.

I used to get up early on weekend mornings and take Benjamin out so that Mom and Daniel could sleep in. As Daniel became older, I would take you boys out early on a weekend morning. My usual routine was to have breakfast at the

◂ ▴ Benjamin and Daniel, Soneva Fushi, Maldives, 2001 and 1999

Starlight Diner in downtown Moscow and then take you boys to buy a balloon at Detsky Mir or the latest pirated Disney DVDs I would buy at a typical Moscow kiosk. If you boys happened to fall asleep, I would drive to my favorite coffee place, lug both of you in your car seats into the coffee shop, and do some reading. When one of you woke up, we would head back home.

One weekend morning, after breakfast, I decided to take Benjamin to the animal market in Moscow. As I look back, it was a bit sad to see how the animals were treated, but on that day Benjamin, less than two years old at that time, was very excited. He focused on the turtles, which were piled on top of each other. That day Benjamin came home with a turtle whom he had named Tommy Turtle. Mom and I got home from going out one day and Benjamin was in the living room playing with Tommy Turtle while Valentina was feeding Daniel. Mom and I realized that Tommy was not moving and had to break the bad news to little Benjamin that Tommy had died.

Benjamin and Daniel, Maldives, 2000

Some months later we were planning a trip to the Maldives, the first of three consecutive annual winter getaway trips to Soneva Fushi in the Maldives. We loved it at Soneva Fushi! It was absolute paradise, particularly in the middle of a Russian winter. The resort had its own island. We deposited our shoes at the front door and did not put them on again until we left, two weeks later. One day Benjamin and I were waiting in the omelet line for breakfast, and there was a very overweight man in front of us. Benjamin asked me, in the loudest voice possible, "Daddy, why does that man have such a big belly?" The man smiled at us.

Right before our first winter trip to the Maldives, in December 1999, a friend of mine from work found a cat that needed a home. Benjamin was most crazy about Teletubbies and cats. He loved to make a cute cat sound. We always thought that was because his first potty trainer was in the shape of a cat, which we called Caca-Kitty. I took Benjamin over to see Bella 1 and we end-

Benjamin and Teletubby, Soneva Fushi, Maldives, 1999

ed up bringing her home. The night before we left for the Maldives we found Bella 1 in Daniel's crib about to scratch little Daniel. Mom and I decided that we needed to get rid of Bella 1, so I took her back early the next morning, without Benjamin knowing, to my friend's house.

All during the trip to the Maldives, Benjamin would say, "I love Bella so much." Mom and I would look at each other as if to say, "What are we going to do?" We called our vet in Moscow from the Maldives, told her the story, and asked her to find a similar-looking cat for us, as our vet had given shots to Bella 1 and knew what she looked like. In Moscow, there was no shortage of cats that needed good homes. It still reminds me of the scene in *Meet the Parents* when Ben Stiller replaces the cat of his soon-to-be-in-laws that he thought he had

Bella 2, the Russian kitty, 1999

lost, and Robert De Niro finds out. This is how Bella 2 came to our family and she was loved by all!

Bella 2 used to especially love when you guys had friends over. She would hang out with you the whole time when you were playing inside. Shortly after we got Bella 2, Mom's friend in London, Rika, told us that she had to get rid of her golden retriever, Muffin, after getting a divorce from her husband and having to move back to Finland. We quickly decided to adopt Muffin, and Mom went to London to pick her up and bring her back. You boys were in love with Muffin right away. She was the sweetest dog ever. Bella was not excited about Muffin initially and spent a good few days upstairs, where Muffin was not allowed.

A few months later, Grandma and Grandpa came to visit us in Moscow. Mom had been in Iowa with them, and they brought back Gryphen, Mom's little toy poodle, so we went quickly from no pets to two dogs and one cat. It was great having Grandma and Grandpa visit, and they enjoyed themselves as well. They actually visited twice, the second time bringing my dad, Papa Dave, with them. We also had visits from Marci and Brian and their girls, Baba Toba, Heidi and Greg and their girls, Karen, Roy and Grace, and Siu Mei. Siu Mei came to visit from Singapore and had a few recollections of her visit: "I just remember being very, very cold, you eating caviar by the spoon out of a gigantic tin, and me being hauled into a Russian police station (and almost had to sit in a jail cell and couldn't reach you to bail me out) because I did not register myself after I arrived in Moscow." Despite being the perfect mother, Mom still had the spirit of adventure and took her friend Karen to Saint Petersburg on the overnight train from Moscow when Karen came to visit. Yes, life in Russia certainly was not boring!

Jackie, Daniel, and Benjamin in Iowa, 1999

the others that
me is one of th
a cane...they are
on the beach.
wooden
a postcard:
the city where
eryone seems to
(+ Mandarin)... the
city is very
"squat" or
Town to
foreign-
Barry.
that

10

Living the Life in Serebryany Bor, Moscow

We really had a great life in Serebryany Bor in Moscow. You guys used to love the swings outside our house and the Moscow River right outside our gate. By that time we had Kiril, our driver; Valentina, your nanny; and Lena, who would clean our house but also spend time with you. It was like we had created our own close nuclear family. You were both so loved with Mom, Lena, and Valentina, plus Kiril, always around.

Benjamin and Daniel, Serebryany Bor, Moscow, 2000

Benjamin and Daniel,
Serebryany Bor, Moscow, 2001

Also, Mom and I had a great social life, making great friends with expats from a number of different countries, particularly Zora and Franck (and their children Markian and Kalina). As usual, Mom made so many close friends, Suzanne, Caterina, Penny, Anya, Dallas, and a number of others. We seemed to always be having some kind of fun party with our Serebryany Bor community, despite raising very small kids. Suzanne gave an example of our social life: "Charlie and Caren Ryan's '80s-themed party (with your dad as Brezhnev and your mom is the one in the disco outfit) and the Skelly's 1920s party. Your parents 'dress like your favorite cocktail' party (not sure which cocktail your parents are dressed as, but your father had a banana on his head) was a great party! I remember people coming as Black Russians, White Russians, margaritas." Actually, I came as a banana daiquiri, which accounts for the banana on my head. Mom went as a Singapore sling.

Daniel, Lena, Valentina, and Benjamin, 2001

Zora and Jackie

Jackie dressed as a Singapore sling at our "come as your own cocktail" party, Moscow, 2000

A favorite yearly event was when all the foreign embassies had dinner dances and you selected the embassy you would go to by lottery. We were awarded the Peruvian Embassy one year and the Swedish Embassy another year. I also very fondly remember seeing the Eagles in concert in Moscow with Mom. We were surprised at how many Russians knew the words to so many of the songs. Most of Mom's closest friends, except for Zora, lived in Serebryany Bor. Suzanne describes Serebryany Bor this way: "We all lived on this island called 'Serebryany Bor,' which is Russian for Silver Woods, due to all the birch trees on the island. It was about a twenty-five-minute drive, without traffic, from Red Square in Central Moscow and an ideal place to live. Half of the 3 x 4 kilometer island was designated as a conservation area (unusual in Moscow) for Muscovites to enjoy, while the other half was residential. It was very difficult to find affordable, legal housing on the island and if you did you considered yourself lucky."

A description of Serebryany Bor appeared in the magazine *Moscow*: "Legend has it that one day Empress Catherine the Great saw forest-covered pines on the bank of the Moscow River and called them Silver Pinewood. Wherever the name comes from, dachas, or summer houses, were established here in the nineteenth century and Muscovite aristocrats and rich merchants were among the first to holiday here in the summer because of its beaches on the Moscow River, its many trees, great rugged beauty."

Our house (dacha) was on Tamanskaya, the main road of the island. Suzanne continues: "Your compound consisted of two new wooden dachas, a tiny old dacha, and then a fantastic, extremely old, full of character, slightly dilapidated blue dacha which was yours. I was invited over to your neighbors'

Our dacha on Serebryany Bor, 2000

Jackie, Kelly, Penny, Suzanne, and Caterina, 2000

one day, the Skellys, and met your mom. She was so welcoming, funny, and interesting. I loved her immediately! Your compound was so active with lots of people coming and going, kids, animals everywhere. From then on, we would spend many days at your compound, with the children playing, laughing at the menagerie of animals going in and out of your house, chatting, sharing thoughts on everything from where to buy difficult-to-come-by products to the best places in the world to live. We went to other friends' compounds on the island as well, but for some reason yours was like a magnet!"

For a bite out, we often went to our favorite, the Starlight Diner, or to the Canadian Bagel shop, Pizza Express, or, for a nice meal, Scandinavia. Over time, our favorites for eating out with friends on a weekend night were the Pushkin restaurant and a Georgian restaurant called Khachapuri.

Benjamin, Jackie, and Daniel with Moscow friends, Sharm el Sheikh, Egypt, 2001

I was always so amazed by how quickly Mom would make deep, deep friendships with really nice women, and they would fall in love with her. Mom and you two and three other friends and their children "hatched a plan" in the middle of winter to go to Sharm El Sheikh, Egypt, for a getaway. As Mom's friend Penny described the trip: "Midwinter in Moscow with little children logically meant a girl's trip to the sunshine. For some reason, we didn't choose the luxury of Dubai, but went on a week trip to Egypt. Jackie, Kelly, Suzanne and I, all with a little child or two in tow. The 5-star hotel was not the luxury promised and was definitely worn around the edges.

"Being a group of women with young children, we didn't rank very highly at all in the waiting staff's priority list for who to serve. I remember us corralling little children into the dining room, a big gang of noise and chaos. We tried to find high chairs, pushed tables together and then sat waiting to be served . . . and we sat waiting and waiting. Strangely, when we arrived the next evening we were warmly greeted by several waiters with open arms and huge toothy smiles. 'Miss Jackie, Miss Jackie,' they cried as they ushered our group to the best table in the house. We all sat bemused by the change in attitude, until Jackie told us point blank that she had dropped a huge tip the previous night and told them more was definitely on its way. Practical Jackie had saved the holiday! We had all been bemoaning the chauvinistic behavior of the waiting staff, only for Jackie to set them to rights with her form of Girl Power. We laughed hysterically that night and every night, of course because Jackie was there."

Mom would remain close with most of them, doing a number of ladies' trips together long after we left Moscow, like the Camino trip they did in Spain in April 2017, which we followed up with our own pilgrimage to honor Mom in May 2018 to Northwest Spain. We also liked our neighbors in our Moscow compound: Martin and Kelly Skelly and their children, Angel and Ann Martin.

One of the stories Mom used to like to tell involved Ann Martin. She was roughly two years old, around the same age as Daniel. One day you kids were playing outside, and Ann Martin had to go no. 2 and could not hold it in. She pulled down her pants and did it right there in the yard, and, unfortunately, Muffin came over and ate it. Muffin had always been the dog that "never did anything wrong" (particularly later when we got Sparrow), but from then on she was "the dog that never did anything wrong, except for eating Ann Martin's poo." There were two other houses in the compound, one rented by an older American couple. The man, I cannot remember his name, worked for a large global brewery that had purchased breweries in Russia. Thus, we were always supplied with beer.

Also, you boys loved our security guard, Alexander, who often played with both of you. There was also a Russian couple who had a boy, Danny, whom you guys played with sometimes. When I asked the dad what he did, he said, "I am a biznessman," code word for Russian Mafia. He was nice to me, but we rarely talked. In fact, the first real conversation I remember having with him was

Martin Skelly and Daniel, 1999

when we were about to leave to move back to the US. He asked me if I wanted to "buy a yacht." Funny!

You boys used to love coming into work with me on Saturday, when the office was closed. You used to run around the trading room and had so much fun, particularly having make-believe conversations on the phones on the trading desks, which you both found so interesting! We would end the visit to my office by going downstairs to McDonald's. (ING occupied the top three floors, and McDonald's was at the ground level.) I remember joking with Benjamin when he asked what I did, and I responded, "I flip burgers." Benjamin, you repeated that to your teacher in the Moscow International School when asked what

Benjamin with security guard Alexander, Serebryany Bor, Moscow, 1999

your dad did. Afterward, you would both sometimes take a nap with Daddy or Mommy in our living room.

Despite arriving in Russia during its worst financial crisis, in 1998, one of the world's biggest market falls (a 90% devaluation of its currency), and political turbulence that threatened to bring the Communist Party, headed then by Gennady Zyuganov, back to power, I was determined to make enough money in Russia to be able to do what I wanted once we left. I had dedicated myself to learning all I could about Russia—its language, culture, and economy—and made some good contacts. I loved immersing myself in "all things Russia" for close to four years. Because so many foreign financial firms had left Russia during the crisis, ING-Barings had a relatively prominent position in the country, which allowed me to develop a number of important relationships with government officials, the Central Bank, and business leaders.

Benjamin and Daniel taking a nap with Dad, Serebryany Bor, 2000

While Putin was still prime minister, I met regularly with his chief of protocol, Vladimir Rakhmanin, whom I had coincidently met at a conference for young financial leaders in Shanghai, China, in 1992. Strangely, shortly after Putin became president, on our last meeting for coffee, Vladimir told me that he would no longer be able to be in contact with me. I also played tennis regularly with Bill Browder, who ran the largest hedge fund in Russia, Hermitage. Bill ultimately became Putin's enemy no. 1 after he dedicated his life to getting sanctions (known as the Magnitsky Act, named after his lawyer) put on a number of important Russian officials in many countries, including the US, after his lawyer was murdered while in prison on trumped-up charges.

I also knew Michael Calvey well. He was an American who founded the first and largest private equity firm in Russia, Barings Vostok. We worked on a couple of projects together. Unfortunately, Mike got caught up in Putin's political, anti-West agenda and is currently in jail in Russia, also on false charges.

I remember the end of December 1999 with so much media hype and attention on Y2K and the issue of whether computers would malfunction or not, with particular concern in Russia over the electrical and nuclear grid, because of how outdated and old the systems were. Russia had one of the few stock markets opened on December 31, 1999. That day, then-president Boris Yeltsin, who was thought to be losing his sanity, announced that he was stepping down from the presidency and was appointing his prime minister, Vladimir Putin, until the upcoming March elections.

At that point, there was a serious concern that the Communist Party would win the elections. Yeltsin had been way behind in the polls for the presidential elections of March 2000. That surprise announcement, and lack of liquidity in the Russian stock market, due to Y2K and so many markets being closed, caused a one-day increase in the market of 25% and a number of Russian companies to increase in value by 100% or more.

With this good news, given our large investments in Russia, Mom and I decided to book a suite at the Kempinsky Hotel and took you boys there to celebrate the New Year's weekend in style. What a wonderful evening with you boys and Mom it was. Right after New Year's, Mom and I decided that we would buy a bigger house in Sausalito. The first house I bought in 1991, which we lived in for a little over one year and took Benjamin back to, was too small for our family.

A real-estate agent started looking for a house for us. After a few months she told me that she had found the perfect house for our family but that I had to see it quickly and, if interested, make an offer because the market was so hot. At first, I thought it ridiculous to travel more than twenty hours from Moscow for a long weekend just to see a house, but after discussing it with Mom, I decided to do just that. I arrived in San Francisco on Saturday and went to the open house on Sunday morning.

I was disappointed! It was a very nice but way too small for our family. As a side note, the well-known author Amy Tan ended up buying the house. Howev-

181 San Carlos Avenue
Sausalito, California

er, on the way out from the open house, I bumped into an elderly woman who asked me what I thought of the house. When I told her my story of looking for a house for our family, she said, "I have a house down the street I will be putting on the market in about six months. I can let you know when it is on the market." I explained that we were living in Moscow and asked if there was any way I could see it. Thankfully, she arranged with her tenants to let me have a quick look.

The house at 181 San Carlos Avenue, Sausalito, was perfect for our family. I spoke with Mom on the phone, and we agreed that I would try to work out a deal with her but leave a contingency for Mom to fly back to see and approve of the house. I had learned from the Moscow experience. Over the next few hours, I sat down with the woman, Naomi, and negotiated a deal. The clincher was that we would let her live rent-free in the property's cottage for two years (or until she found a new place). Because we were still planning to live in Moscow for two more years, and ended up doing so, it was no big deal for us to let her live in the cottage.

Mom traveled back to San Francisco one week later to see the house. She loved it, and this helped cement our plans to move back to Sausalito in a few years. It is called the Pilot House as it was owned by the harbormaster of Sausalito in the early 1900s when there were few houses in Sausalito. We had a place where we were greatly looking forward to raising a family! Around that time, we also decided to purchase an apartment in Moscow, more as an investment and fun renovation project. I had one stipulation—it had to have a "drop-dead" gorgeous view of Saint Basil's Cathedral, which still today, along with the Taj Mahal, ranks as one of the most beautiful buildings I have ever seen. In those days, it was actually legal for foreigners to own property in Moscow according to the Moscow city government regulations, but not yet legal for foreigners to own property according to federal government regulations.

We knew we were taking a risk in buying an apartment, but all investments in Russia, in those days, were about measuring risk and making the decision whether you were appropriately compensated for that risk. It took a while, but we found the apartment we wanted to buy. It was exactly what I was looking for: small, two bedrooms, unimpeded view of Saint Basil's Cathedral. In Soviet times, the Communist government allocated apartments, partly based on your ranking in the Communist Party. If you did not like your apartment or your family situation changed, too bad.

The backstory for the apartment we purchased was interesting. The apartment had been allocated to a young couple in the 1970s, during Communist times. The couple had a child, who, by the time we purchased the apartment, was in his late twenties. The couple had become estranged in the early 1980s and actually divorced, but because they had been unable to switch apartments,

Daniel and Benjamin, St. Basil's Cathedral, Moscow, 2002

they all continued to live together until they decided to sell the apartment. We purchased the apartment for $60,000. With that amount, the family then bought three other apartments in the suburbs of Moscow: one for the son, one for the mother, and one for the father. In those days, there was no such thing as escrow for real estate. I had to hire a lawyer to verify all documents. I also had to get the entire family to obtain a medical certificate that said they were mentally capable of making the decision to sell the apartment.

Finally, we met at the bank where we were to exchange money for the apartment. But because the sellers were buying three other apartments simultaneously, the three other sellers met at the same time. I gave them the $60,000 all in cash (which I had carried in a bag), and they used a machine to ensure the authenticity of the bills. They gave $20,000 each to of the owners who were selling them the apartments, and they went through the same procedure in verifying the authenticity of the bills. The whole process was a bit convoluted but interesting and took something like six hours. Shortly thereafter, we began a big remodel project in which we completely renovated the entire apartment for something like $20,000 and ended up with a really beautiful apartment. We stayed there a few times and let friends stay there. After about six months, we rented the apartment out to an expat who lived there the next six years until I returned to Moscow in 2006 and sold it.

While in Moscow, we did get to travel a good bit. Every year I had to renew my work visa, which entailed going to another country and picking up the new work visa. Most of my foreign colleagues did that in London, but Mom and I used that occasion to travel with you boys to Estonia and Latvia in successive years. I remember you boys running, with so much energy, up and down the halls, late at night, in our hotel in Tallinn, the capital of Estonia. We also did some travel around Russia and again to Saint Petersburg. We took a few trips to some of the Golden Ring towns not far from Moscow: Yaroslavl, Ivanovo, Vladimir, Sergiev Posad, and particularly Suzdal. We went there with Zora and Franck and their family and also Marci and Brian and their girls. These are all UNESCO World Heritage towns—picturesque open-air museums full of historic kremlins, monasteries, and cathedrals that typify Russian architecture from the twelfth to eighteenth century.

Jackie and Daniel, 2001

The following year, when Benjamin turned three, Mom and some neighbors decided to start a little preschool in the upstairs room in our house in Serebryany Bor. They hired a Russian woman to teach the school in both Russian and English. Though Daniel was only a year and a half, he attended as well. This went on for about one year, three days a week for four hours a day.

The following year we enrolled Benjamin in the American International School. It was definitely strange to be taking you to school, entering the same front door as all the other students even up to grade 12. I remember the first day. You were quite scared and hid behind my legs. However, you quickly adjusted and made some nice friends, particularly Pauly and Andrew. Daniel, your closest friend was Marcus, Mom's Australian friend Caterina's older son.

BARRY'S EASTERN EUROPE WORK TRAVELS

1. MOSCOW, RUSSIA
2. KIEV, UKRAINE
3. BUDAPEST, HUNGARY
4. BUCHAREST, ROMANIA
5. SOFIA, BULGARIA
6. BRATISLAVA, SLOVAKIA
7. PRAGUE, CZECH REPUBLIC
8. WARSAW, POLAND
9. ISTANBUL, TURKEY
10. BELGRADE, SERBIA

The Anglo-American School of Moscow
First Trimester Specialist Report
Phone:(7) (095) 231 – 4482 Email: aasls@online.ru

STUDENT NAME: Benjamin Hoffner
GRADE: PRE-K HOMEROOM TEACHER: Horton
MUSIC Khvatova

Course Content	Narrative
Singing Skills Group In-tune Singing with approximate pitches, songs are based on pentatonic "drmsl" Rhythmic Skills Steady beat, Rhythm Patterns, differences in Fast-Slow movement Aural Perception High-Low, Soft-loud relationships, differentiation between contrast sounds. Music Listening Listening for content Playing Percussion Instruments Group/Alone Steady Beat	Benjamin listens attentively and participates actively. He sings with skill, moves to the beat/rhythm, plays instruments with skill, and recognizes musical patterns.

Benjamin's first progress report, Anglo-American School, Moscow, 2001

At that point, my responsibilities at work had increased and I was traveling all over Eastern Europe two or three days a week between Kiev, Warsaw, Prague, Bratislava, Sofia, Bucharest, and Istanbul. While at first I enjoyed traveling and meeting my local teams in each country, learning about their businesses and culture, I was missing you boys and Mom. You guys would run up and give me the biggest hugs when I got home from a trip, and I would always have something for you. On one trip, Daniel, I brought you a lollipop shaped as a train. You called it "Chu-Chu Aku." After that, whenever I asked you what you wanted when I went away, you would say, "I want Chu-Chu Aku!" Much as I looked, I could not find additional lollipops in the shape of a train, but one time I did find these massive lollipops that you guys loved!

Don't get me wrong, I loved my job. I worked with some great colleagues, Max, Sergey, Elena, Vika, and so on, and had some tremendous work expe-

Benjamin and Daniel with lollipops, Serebryany Bor, 2002

riences, but the travel was wearing on me. It was a pain to go in and out of Sheremetyevo Airport in Moscow each week. On one of my trips, Mom surprised me. I had to be in Bratislava on Friday; meet a client for breakfast in Vienna on Saturday morning; and then go to Sofia on Monday morning. So I asked Mom if she minded if I stayed the weekend in Vienna to catch up on some stuff and principally to rest. Late Friday night I heard a knock on my hotel room door, opened it up, and there was sweet Mom with a bottle of champagne and two glasses. We spent a wonderful weekend in Vienna while you guys stayed with Lena and Valentina. Mom and I also managed to attend Roy and Grace's wedding in Singapore in 2000 and traveled to Uzbekistan in 2001 (so I could knock off another leg of the Silk Road). I am sure you guys missed us, but we knew you were in the best of hands with Valentina

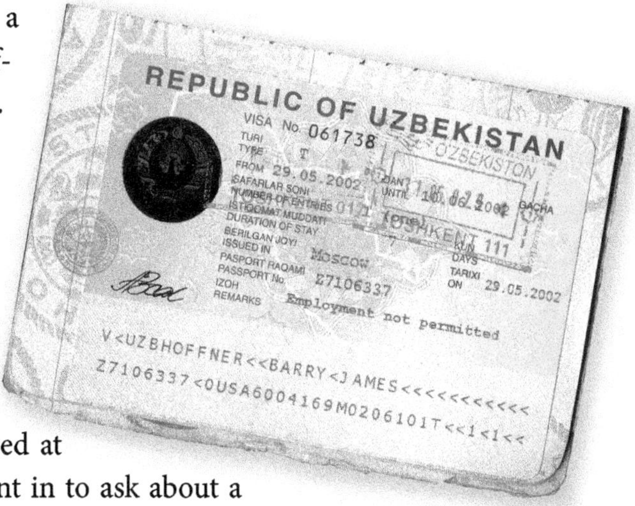

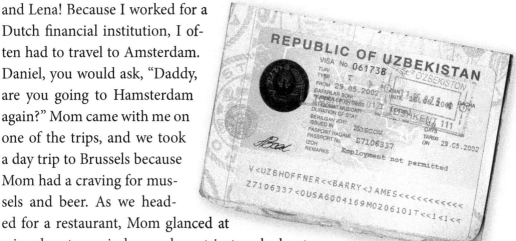

and Lena! Because I worked for a Dutch financial institution, I often had to travel to Amsterdam. Daniel, you would ask, "Daddy, are you going to Hamsterdam again?" Mom came with me on one of the trips, and we took a day trip to Brussels because Mom had a craving for mussels and beer. As we headed for a restaurant, Mom glanced at a jewelry store window and went in to ask about a particular ring but decided not to get it. On the train trip back to Amsterdam from Brussels, I felt bad about not encouraging her to get it. Two weeks later I had to travel, again, to Amsterdam on business. I decided that I needed to surprise Mom with that ring; however, I knew neither the name of the store nor exactly where it was. I did find that store, but it was closed. I went into the adjacent shop and inquired about the owner of the jewelry store. The clerk put me in touch with the owner who promptly came to the shop and sold me the ring. I was quite proud of my little adventure and the ring that I procured for Mom, and she was pleased as well.

For my 40th birthday, I decided that I wanted to take my whole family to Israel. I was usually the planner of family trips but messed up on this one. As we were driving in traffic toward the airport in Moscow, I realized that I had left our tickets at home. There was simply no way to go back, grab the tickets, and get to the airport on time. Thus, I had to "eat" those tickets and purchase last-minute tickets to Tel Aviv later that night. This was the first of a number of mishaps on the trip that we named "the nightmare fortieth birthday trip."

Mom asked me what I wanted most to do while I was in Israel and I said taking my sons to the Western Wall. However, the next morning Daniel was not feeling so well so I decided to take only Benjamin. When I went to get you, you said, in Russian, "Tolka momi" (Only Mom). This became our joke for a number of years. The next night was my actual birthday, and we were staying at the King David Hotel. I told Mom that I wanted to go to a well-known Arabic restaurant in East Jerusalem, but Mom said that she had already organized my birthday dinner. So after a long day out, we got home to the birthday dinner the hotel had set out for us. Unfortunately, because it was the week of Passover and the King David kept kosher, there were only a few things to eat, like a cheese platter and some vegetables. We laughed about that as well. Two nights later we were driving to see our friends Iris and Eran, whom Mom and I had met in China. They had invited us for Passover dinner. Daniel started crying and was in clear distress. We diverted straight to the hospital where we learned that Daniel had a bowel obstruction, and we spent most of the evening in the hospital. Two days later we were at a restaurant in Tel Aviv only to find out after lunch that our car had been towed. We definitely made the best of it, but it was a challenging trip for sure!

Because ING was the depository and registrar for all Russian stocks that were issued as American depositary receipts (ADRs), ING was responsible for representing foreign shareholders at shareholder meetings. Right after the financial crisis in 1998, Russian financial companies learned the worst things about how to legally take advantage of foreign shareholders in financial markets by calling shareholder meetings and diluting minority shareholders by issuing new stock. There was not much that we, as foreign investors, could do.

I happened to be in Sofia, Bulgaria, the day of the 9/11 attacks and will never forget running on a treadmill in the hotel gym, and looking up at the TV to see on CNN live the plane crashing into the World Trade Center. The next morning, I had to fly to Bucharest, Romania, but could not bring myself to go to the ING office that day. I remember sitting in my hotel room watching CNN all day, completely stunned! I was beginning to tire of so much traveling. People were still on edge after the 9/11 attacks. Then only weeks later, I was in Kiev, Ukraine, on business ready to return to Moscow and arrived at the airport to learn that all flights were canceled for the next few days. The Ukraine Air Force mistakenly shot down a Siberia Airlines flight to Israel over the Black Sea. All passengers aboard, close to seventy people, were dead. I took a taxi to the Kiev train station and bought an overnight ticket to travel back to Moscow by train.

On that train ride, I decided I had enough of the travel! Being so far away from home, for quite a number of years at that point, Mom and I had a serious discussion about future plans and decided to return home in 2002. We had the house we purchased at 181 San Carlos Avenue in Sausalito rented out to tenants and told them that we would be moving back in about six months.

11

Leaving Moscow, Russia (June 2002)

Having decided that we would move back to the US in 2002, I gave notice at work that I would stay until mid-2002. We made a trip back home for the holidays in late 2001, at which time we secured a preschool for you boys at the Early Childhood Education (ECE) in San Rafael.

Thus, our new direction was set—we were leaving Russia in June 2002 to start a new life in our new house in Sausalito. It was definitely bittersweet. We were greatly looking forward to our next chapter as a family but also sad to be leaving Moscow, where we raised our family, had some incredible experiences, acquired some pets, and made some amazing friends, including some very special Russians like Valentina, Lena, and Kiril. Nonetheless, we were also looking forward to being closer to family (mine and Mom's).

Suzanne wrote: "Your mom had great nannies who would help her with the house and the boys. After spending a week with your family, they would become more like long-lost sisters. Your mom treated them so well! I thought I would love to work as a nanny for your family."

What an amazing time our four years in Moscow were. I remember those years so fondly and always will. To start, just raising you boys in such an interesting place, with such great care from Mom and our nuclear family, close friends, and a great lifestyle. I have so many great memories from those years that will last a lifetime.

Russia was in a fast pace of change from communism to capitalism and then, just before we left, toward authoritarianism. When we arrived in Moscow, the nation had one of the most open and democratic presses in the world.

Baba Toba's 90th birthday, San Francisco, California, 2011

Its political process, while chaotic, was also very open. With the economy in transition from state-owned to commercial, the economic model was a very interesting one. There were a lot of challenges living in Moscow—the weather in winter; the frequent harshness and coldness of some Russians, particularly the authorities; the traffic in Moscow; and so on. As Suzanne said, "Raising babies in Moscow wasn't always an easy task, especially in the early days. . . . What is Russian for low-fat sour cream? Which shops sold wet wipes? Where could I send my children to school?" Despite these challenges, it was such an impactful and consequential time in our lives.

I had been working out a lot and decided that before leaving Moscow, I would attempt to climb Mount Elbrus, the highest mountain in Europe, in the Caucasus Mountains in Russia, at an elevation of 18,510 feet. Mom and I had a great Russian trainer, Patrick, at our gym near Serebryany Bor, who helped me get in shape for Elbrus.

He was an animal in terms of training and had very strange methods for getting people into shape. I can definitely say that he got me from the most

Hoffner family at our house at Serebryany Bor, Moscow, 1999

unfit I had been (from working in a building that had McDonald's on the bottom floor and taking you guys there, your favorite place) to the best shape of my life.

Mom used to like to tell the story of how she met Patrick. Mom was walking moderately on the treadmill, and Patrick came up and said, "If that is how you are going to work out, why bother coming to the gym? Mom did not take offense, because that was Patrick's personality.

For squats he used to like to jump on top of people he was training and then make them do squats! Mom and I loved going to the gym and would meet there regularly on my way home from work, before Valentina returned home for the evening. We even stayed for some sushi at the gym's lounge, which had some of the best sushi in Moscow. Mom's friend Suzanne described the gym this way:

Barry on Mount Elbrus, the Caucasus, Russia, 2002

"The Valery Sports Club had fantastic swimming pools, tennis courts, and exercise facilities. Most of the expat families we knew joined the club and during the day often took the children to swim in the pools, particularly during winter."

Anticipating leaving Moscow was tough. We had such a great quality of life, we lived in an interesting place, I had a great job, we had great friends, you guys were very content, Valentina, Kiril, and Lena were like family, and it was a special time in our lives. Suzanne described what it was like for the moms: "Moscow was a special place for all the expats with young children, especially for the mothers who tended to stay at home. Typically, most of us would have had a good job outside the home; however, given the circumstances (language barriers, complicated domestic situations, and visa issues), many of us found ourselves in a very foreign land without much to do except take care of our children. In a way, this was fortuitous as it meant that there were many educated, interesting, lively women who were all facing the same circumstances without the support of relatives or old friends. I've always said that Moscow was a funny place in those days, in terms of making friends . . . you would meet someone on a Tuesday at baby group, have happy hour with them on Friday, and then by the following week they would be one of your best friends. Friendships were quickly made with very tight bonds."

Aside from trips with the family and to other countries in Eastern Europe where ING-Barings had offices, I did manage to take a few interesting trips while in Russia:

Krasnoyarsk, Siberia, Russia (Midwinter 2001)

I remember one interesting trip before the Russian presidential elections of 2000, traveling to Krasnoyarsk, Siberia, in the middle of winter with ING's Global Head of Emerging Markets Research, Ron Neumunz, to interview one of the more well-known presidential candidates, General Alexander Lebed, a very scary guy! He placed third in the presidential elections with 14% of the vote and then became governor of the Krasnoyarsk region, until he died in a helicopter crash in 2002. I learned what it meant to be cold, and that is when the Fahrenheit temperature and the Celsius temperature meet, which is at -40 degrees. It was that temperature during our stay in Krasnoyarsk. To top this interesting trip off, on the return flight from Krasnoyarsk to Moscow, my colleague Ron woke me up mid-flight and pointed at the floor. A live alligator was in the aisle not more than ten feet from us. It created a bit of chaos on the plane. A passenger had tried to smuggle an alligator into Moscow to sell in the animal market and had put it in a tube and wrapped it in tape, but it got out.

Murmansk, Russia (Summer 2000)

Murmansk sits close to 200 miles above the Arctic Circle whereas Anchorage, Alaska, for example, is well below it. With a population of around three hundred thousand, Murmansk is the largest and most populated northernmost

BARRY'S RUSSIAN ADVENTURES

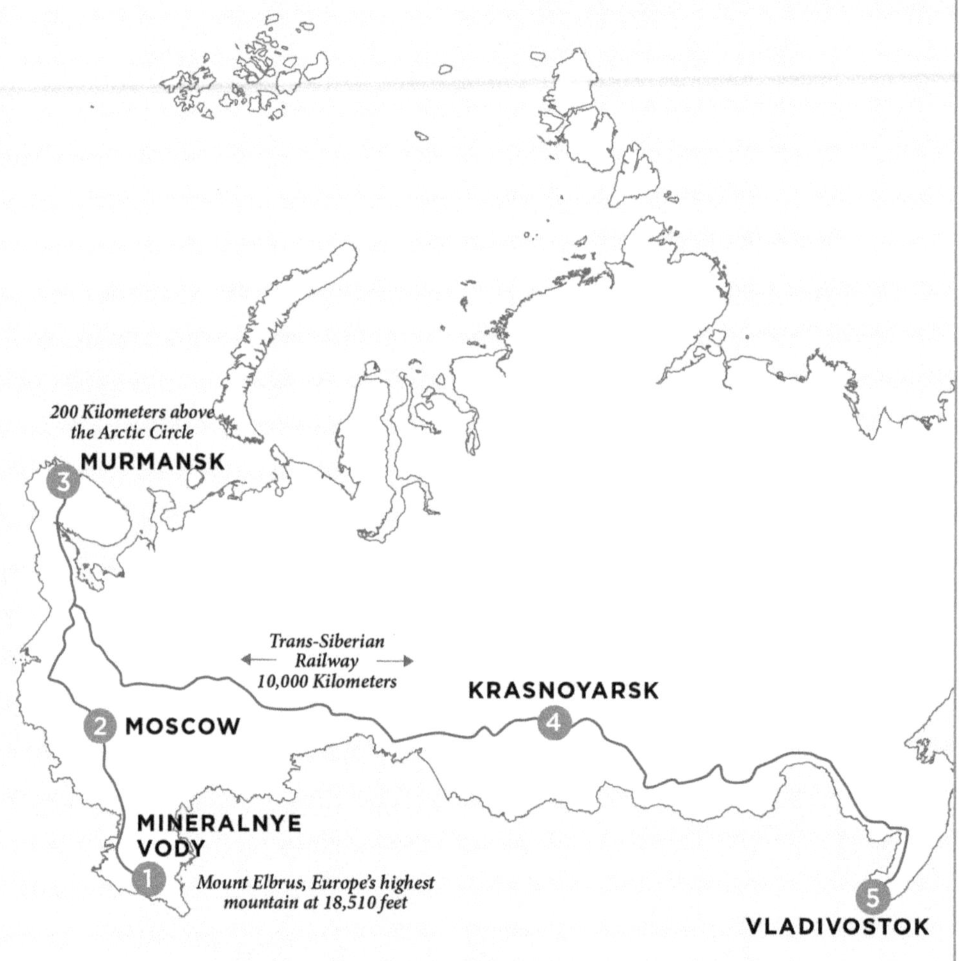

city in the world, sitting at 68 degrees latitude. Despite being above the Arctic Circle and surrounded by the Arctic Ocean, the city has a mostly ice-free port, making it one of Russia's most important naval ports. While I have never been much of a "guy's guy," a group of guys I knew in Moscow, some American, others Russian, invited me to go fly-fishing in Russia's arctic region. We flew from Moscow to Murmansk and then took an old, dilapidated Russian military helicopter from Murmansk to the place where we would spend the next few days. Since it was early summer, we never saw the sun set. The sun was even visible at midnight. The briefing we were given was as follows:

- Never take off your mosquito fishing mask when outside
- Liberally apply Deet
- Drink as much vodka as you want (they brought 2 full cases of vodka)
- Sleep when you are tired, as it will never get even close to dark, i.e., the actual time of day or night means nothing

All went well until a few of the Russians got very drunk, took out their rifles, and started shooting into the woods. We did end up catching some salmon, and it was a very cool experience, but I was happy to get home without any major mishaps. I saw firsthand how much Russians can drink as we returned without a single bottle of vodka.

Mount Elbrus (Summer of 2002)

Back in the 1990s, I was inspired by mountain climbing. I enjoyed the idea of being in the outdoors but with a very focused goal of getting to the top of the mountain. I enjoyed the camaraderie and support of those climbing together. Thus I figured it would be a fitting end to my life-changing four years in Russia to summit Europe's highest peak (18,510 feet) located not just in Russia but in the Caucasus Mountains, a very interesting and historical place in itself. The Caucasus region has a documented history dating back at least 1,000 years BC, and as part of the Persian Empire starting 500 years BC. It is home to multiple ethnic groups, mostly Muslim, with the Chechens being the most well-known. Some very intense fighting took place between Russia and Germany high up in the Caucasus Mountains in World War II. The Caucasus also played an important role in Putin getting elected as president of Russia because of his launch of all-out war with Chechnya in late 1999, which resulted in the complete destruction of Grozny, the Chechen capital.

I joined a small group of climbers who spent ten days climbing in the Caucasus Mountains with the goal of reaching the summit of Mount Elbrus, which was less than a two-hour drive from Grozny. While the mountains were absolutely spectacular and I was thrilled to summit Mount Elbrus, I also greatly enjoyed spending time in this region. It had a very interesting culture despite the ongoing challenges with Russia proper.

Trans-Siberian Railway across Russia

For tax reasons locally, I still needed to spend about forty more days in Russia. Although it was hard being away from you guys and Mom, I made the best of this unique adventure, particularly at my age and with my whole family back home. I landed in Vladivostok, Russia (Russia's Far East near Korea) and took a series of train rides all the way to Moscow, a distance of almost 10,000 kilometers, the world's longest railway journey. The Trans-Siberian does the trip straight through in roughly one week. But I decided to stop off along the way and see different places in Siberia, starting in Russia's easternmost city, Vladivostok. I also visited Khabarovsk; Irkutsk to see Lake Baikal, the world's largest freshwater lake by volume (contains more than 20% of the entire world's freshwater); Krasnoyarsk; Novosibirsk; and Yekaterinburg before arriving in Moscow. It was quite an adventure! It seemed as if each of my train compartment roommates always were wanting me to swig a few shots of vodka, and I often ran out of excuses. The two impressions I had of this journey were, wow, Russia has a lot of trees and Russians drink a lot of vodka!

While I was climbing Mount Elbrus, you guys went with Aunt Julie, Bradley, and Nathan to Italy and stayed at Il Crocicchio, an "agriturismo" near Florence in Tuscany, a place we would go back to a couple of times, even on our last family trip to Italy in the summer of 2017.

Visits to Il Crocicchio, Tuscany, Italy

(top) Daniel and Benjamin, 2002; (bottom) Benjamin, Daniel, Nathan and Bradley, 2002

Hoffner family, 2004

(left) Daniel and Benjamin, 2004; (right) Daniel and Benjamin, 2017

12/10
Mrs.
Aunt
Vicki made
GAP
GAP

12

Transition to Sausalito, Final Round

Moving back to Sausalito was bittersweet. We missed our life and friends in Moscow. Mom had been pregnant, and we found out only a few weeks after moving back that we had lost the baby. We were sad but wanted to put on a happy face for you both as you only recently had arrived in California. Grandma and Grandpa were a huge help to us, going to Sausalito before we returned from Moscow to receive Muffin, Gryphen, and Bella, who traveled ahead of us.

Because we were in the middle of remodeling our house at 181 San Carlos, we moved into the cottage. It was definitely interesting with two dogs and a cat

Benjamin, Muffin, and Daniel, in the cottage, Sausalito, California, 2003

Daniel and Benjamin at their first Halloween in Sausalito, California, 2002

plus the four of us in the 900-square-foot cottage, particularly as we got into the rainy months without a fenced-in yard for Muffin to run around. But it was cozy and, as usual, Mom made it all work for us. You guys started school at the ECE in San Rafael in September 2002.

I remember our first Halloween in Sausalito going trick-or-treating on Caledonia Street. You both dressed up in Harry Potter costumes. Shortly after Halloween, I was in Russia for six weeks. It was the first time I was away from the family for such a long stretch, and it was tough. I was very happy to get back in November and begin our life together as a family in Sausalito.

Jackie and Daniel in Sausalito, 2003

Benjamin's first project in nursery school was the 100 days project. Each student in Gimel, the last year of nursery school at the ECE, had to do a poster of 100 of something to represent the first 100 days of school. At that point, I used to take you boys, Muffin, and sometimes Gryphen to the dog park in Sausalito in the late afternoon. Mom would often join us. You guys loved all the dogs. Mom had clearly imprinted her love of animals equally on you both. With a bit of coaching from me, Benjamin took 100 pictures of dogs, got their names from the owners, and put them on a poster. Your favorite dog was a beagle we saw regularly, and you boys asked if we could get one. My answer was that if you still were interested in having a beagle in one year, Mom and I would get a beagle for the family. This is how we came to get Sparrow from a breeder in Colorado. Sparrow became such an important part of our family, and you and your friends received a world of joy from his funny personality! Sparrow and Muffin became the best of friends!

Daniel at Slide Ranch, 2003

Daniel, you demonstrated your great sense of humor early in life when you were handed a banana at snack time your first week at nursery school at the ECE. You said, "No thanks, I have a banana in Moscow!"

In 2003, we made a decision that would play a big role in our lives when we purchased the first parcel of our ranch in Cloverdale. I say big decision because, as you know, the ranch has played an outsized role in our lives. We spent many, many weekends there while you guys were growing up, a place of refuge from our busy life in Sausalito. We shared the ranch with many of our friends and family regularly. Mom loved to entertain up there. In fact, for many years, when you were both at Brandeis Marin, one of the favorite days of the year for both your classes was the field trip to Silverwood Ranch.

Sparrow and Muffin at Silverwood Ranch, Cloverdale, California, 2004

Benjamin and Daniel with Gryphen, Sparrow, and Muffin, 2006

Daniel and Benjamin with Katrina at Silverwood Ranch, Cloverdale, California, 2004

Both of you were bar-mitzvahed at the ranch. As you guys grew up and spent a bit less time at the ranch, Mom and I created our own community of friends and spent a good amount of time there. Having bought the first parcel of the ranch in 2003, we decided, shortly thereafter, to sell the house we owned with Marci and Brian in Lake Tahoe, at Incline Village. We were going there much less frequently. You both took your first ski lesson at Diamond Peak right near our house.

Despite having the ranch as our favorite place to go, dear Mom and I prioritized showing you two the world. We did at least one big trip per year starting the year after we returned home:

2004: London, Paris, Switzerland, Italy
2005: Rogue River, Oregon
2006: Costa Rica

Daniel and Benjamin at Silverwood Ranch, Cloverdale, California, 2008

Boys' bar mitzvah at Silverwood Ranch, Cloverdale, California

Jackie and Gryphen, Kathryn, and Lizzie, Diamond Peak, Lake Tahoe

2007: New Zealand
2008: Ecuador
2009: Japan
2010: Singapore, Thailand, Cambodia, Japan
2011: Lisbon, Mali, Israel
2012: Hawaii
2013: Bermuda, Saint Vincent and the Grenadines, Grenada
2015: Chile
2016: Cuba
2017: Italy (Rome, Tuscany, and Sicily)

I feel confident in saying that travel has been very beneficial in your lives, as it was for Mom and me. It has informed who you are, your sense of adventure, your open-mindedness to think differently about our world and respect people of different cultures despite their level of material wealth. Benjamin, we got you your first passport when you were only a few months old, and it was valid for five years. By the time the passport expired, in 2002, when you were only five years old, shortly after we moved to Sausalito, you had over ninety stamps in your passport (mostly in and out of both England and Russia) from fourteen countries. Daniel, you were not far behind. Travel, adventure, and foreign cultures have definitely educated you, and that is a good thing!

Mom and I also had some memorable trips together when Grandma and Grandpa were able to come and stay with the two of you. We went to Paris and London (to celebrate my friend Hans's fiftieth birthday party at the Hampton Court Palace, outside London), to Italy a few times, once to see James Taylor in concert in Rome, and to New York. On our trip to London and Paris, in 2010, when Mom returned a day earlier than I did (when you guys were young, she was adamant about our flying separately when only the two of us traveled together), I spent my last night in the Ladbroke Arms pub, our favorite pub when we lived in London both times.

That trip had been the most wonderful, action-packed trip with Mom, as a few years earlier we had come out of the more difficult years in our marriage. While eating there alone, in late spring 2010, I wrote Mom a letter, one of the

Ladbroke Arms, London, England

more meaningful letters of my life, on the back a Wagamama dessert menu. It read: "6:30pm Ladbroke Arms, London, England: I am sitting in the Ladbroke Arms, drinking a pint, waiting to order dinner. I am thinking of you a lot today, all nice thoughts I assure you. . . . So much that it kind of hurts a bit. Est-ce que cas c'est le vrai amour je me demande? Oui, je le crois! (Is that true love I ask myself? Yes, I think so!). What a whirlwind! Arriving in London, jet-lagged, to a note for me to call you! I go to sleep unsure of whether or not I will see you in London the next day because of problems with your ticket. You arrive, I organize a "surprise tour," Wagamama, Ladbroke Arms, Orielles, all places where I have great memories of my life in London with you. We walk through the Heath from Hampstead to Highgate to Tadpole Cottage.

Barry and Jackie, Hampton Court Palace, London, 2010

"Another place with great memories of little Benjamin growing up! Check out the London Museum, a walk through Hyde Park and back for dinner with Cynthia and Allan. So great to hang out with friends with an 'outside Marin' perspective. I remember taking the London tube with you for Saturday morning coffee in Hampstead and then off to Chelsea for lunch with Cahn. On the tube, I am holding your hand, and looking deeply into your eyes and feeling so peaceful and so much love in my full heart. A quick visit with Laure and then we take you to some a spiritual healing session with Ann Jones. A walk to Knightsbridge, dinner at a great Lebanese restaurant, back to the hotel to change into formal wear for the big event, Hans's 50th b-day party at some castle. Great atmosphere, great conversation . . . and (et puis en peu l'amour encore)! Sunday off to Paris and staying on Île Saint Louis, walking everywhere, what great dinners we had in Paris. I can't remember the last time we ate so well. Morning coffees at the edge of the island overlooking Notre Dame. I remember the little doggie at the café sitting so contentedly on your lap.

"Then the train back to London to have our last dinner before you leave, a very special dinner at our Ladbroke Arms (where I came back to tonight). What a great trip with you, great company . . . I am still soaking it all in! Jackie, we have been through so much of our lives together. I have known you now almost 30 years (28 to be exact). It has been more than 20 years since I tried to plant a kiss on you, and then your intriguing trip to visit me in NY with your then boyfriend. It has been 15 years since those incredibly magical times with you in India and China, Laos, Thailand and Burma, but particularly India . . . for me almost like a fairy-tale come true. We have been married now for more than 12 years. We have had some amazing times and also some challenges, as every couple goes through. I think it is a testament to us that we have made the effort to work through the challenges, which has led to us moving our marriage to an even higher level. I know there are so many good times ahead of us and also likely some challenges along the way . . . but I believe that we have so much to look forward to together both as a family and as a married couple. With love, Your Hubby."

As you know, Mom was not much of a list person, but she did manage to make a list of things that we accomplished together as a family in the anniversary card she wrote to me in February 2004, roughly a year and a half after arriving in Sausalito from Moscow. The list she notes as follows:

1. Benjamin born Sept. 9th, 1997.
2. Moved to London, Dec. 1997.
3. Move to Moscow, Aug. 1998.
4. Daniel born April 8th, 1999.
5. Moved to Dacha in Serebryany Bor in Moscow in May 1999.
6. Went to Maldives for the first time in winter 2000.
7. You turned 40 in April 2000, and we celebrated in Israel.
8. Winter 2001, another Maldives trip.

9. Summer 2002, moved to Sausalito in 181 San Carlos house.
10. 2003 bought ranch in Cloverdale.

"We had many, many wonderful times here and abroad and look how wonderful our two boys are! I'm looking forward to building on what we already have . . . celebrating many more Valentines/Anniversaries and enjoying many more memories with you, my true love and my hubby. Love, Jackie."

I think I will end this part of our story here. By this time, Benjamin, you were around five years old, and, Daniel, you were going on four and you likely remember most of your life after that, living in Sausalito.

I hope from this story you feel a sense of the deep love I have for your mom that will never go away, a love that started in December 1994 in India. That love has so many facets, not just for your dear mom, but also for you both, obviously, and for our family.

We lost Mom way too soon, and there will always be a hole in our hearts. However, I also know that we were blessed to have traveled the path we did, first Mom and I, and then as a family, and that these memories will never leave us. Through my own personal journey of grieving and attempted healing, I think a lot about the words to that song that I listened to on the plane in the days that followed Mom's passing: "I have faith in what I see, now I know I have met an angel, in person, and she looks perfect."

As you both know, it will always be painful to think about Mom not being physically with us. However, I also know that thinking of never having had Mom in my life is itself also very painful to contemplate.

Everything good that has happened in my own life happened because of Mom. I also know that I have learned so much from her and am still learning, mostly about what it means to be a good human being. I have worked at it and am still working. To Mom, it came naturally. As I have said to Aunt Julie, "There are so many areas where I wish I could be more like your sister." I know I have lived using my head a lot in the past . . . I must honor Mom by using my heart more fully! That will be dear Mom's most important legacy to me. While Mom had so many amazing qualities, physical beauty, kindness, compassion, intelligence, humor, maybe the thing I will always carry with me most is that Mom was someone to believe in and trust in fully! I carry great strength from this. I will also always carry the tremendous pride I have in being Mom's husband, and I am quite sure you feel the same about being her sons. It gives me so much comfort to see your love for animals and reminds me so much of Mom and all she did to give love to, care for, and advocate on behalf of so many different animals, massive and tiny, up until her final days. Finally, I also hope you will agree that the best thing we can do to honor Mom, in a way that she deserves, is for us to stay tight as a family, live worthy lives, love each other, and as much as we can try to emulate dear Mom's open heart full of kindness and compassion, and to know that, surely, she is smiling down on us with her abundant love. I know she is!

I love you both and Mom more than you could ever possibly comprehend.

LOVE, DAD

JACKIE'S DIARIES

As I mentioned in the preface, my original intention was simply to record, for my boys, some of the amazing travel experiences I had with my dear wife in the eighteen-month period from the end of 1994 until mid-1996. I was thinking of perhaps a chronology of ten pages recounting our travels supplemented with a few stories that I could recall. My plans changed the day I found dear Jackie's diaries that she kept when we were traveling. We had not even mentioned those diaries for at least twenty years. As I was reading them at home, fasting for Yom Kippur, 2018, a clear vision came to me that I had to make this into a bigger project, first for my boys, but also for close friends and family . . . but most of all, to keep alive the memories of my dear wife. This story gives me some comfort that, though her life was cut short so tragically, Jackie had a good life. Other than being a good father to my boys, nothing is more important to me than keeping Jackie close to me and her memories alive, and I hope this book does just that. I am therefore including a selection of pages from her diary and also the letter I wrote her from the Ladbrooke Arms on the dessert menu, which I also found with her diaries.

Singapore. 11/23/94

I am sitting in Barry's house at his dining room table. Downstairs, the floors are marble. Upstairs, they are wood. The house is beautiful and he has filled it with Asian relics that describe the past several years of his life in the East. On the walls, he has hung photographs of his journey through China (I've forgotten what part he travelled through)... all of the photographs are of people... most of them children... and they look as if a photographer from National Geographic took them. In front of me is one of four children, sitting together on a bench. The background is grey cobble stone. Three of the children are dressed in shades of red... majenta... orange. The other child is in tan, and is the only one looking into the camera. It must be cold where the photo was taken because all of the children are wearing trousers + thick sweaters + have their heads wrapped in

scarves. Their ethnicity resembles more
Moslem or Eastern European than Chinese.
It is a wonderful photograph ... as are
the others that adorn the walls. Behind
me is one of three older men ... one has
a cane ... they are engaged in conversation
on the beach. In the foreground are two
wooden beach chairs.

As I look around his place, I am
realizing why people have children ... Barry
should have a child ... because someday that
child would look over these photographs
that his father had taken and realize
the richness in this man's life ... the
adventure he had, and the genuine love
he possessed for Asia. He is not consumed
by it, but it does border passion ...

I envy Barry, and I love him dearly.
He left this morning for the States, to visit
his family. I miss him very much. I
am here now with Vicki ... and she misses
him, too. We went to China Town

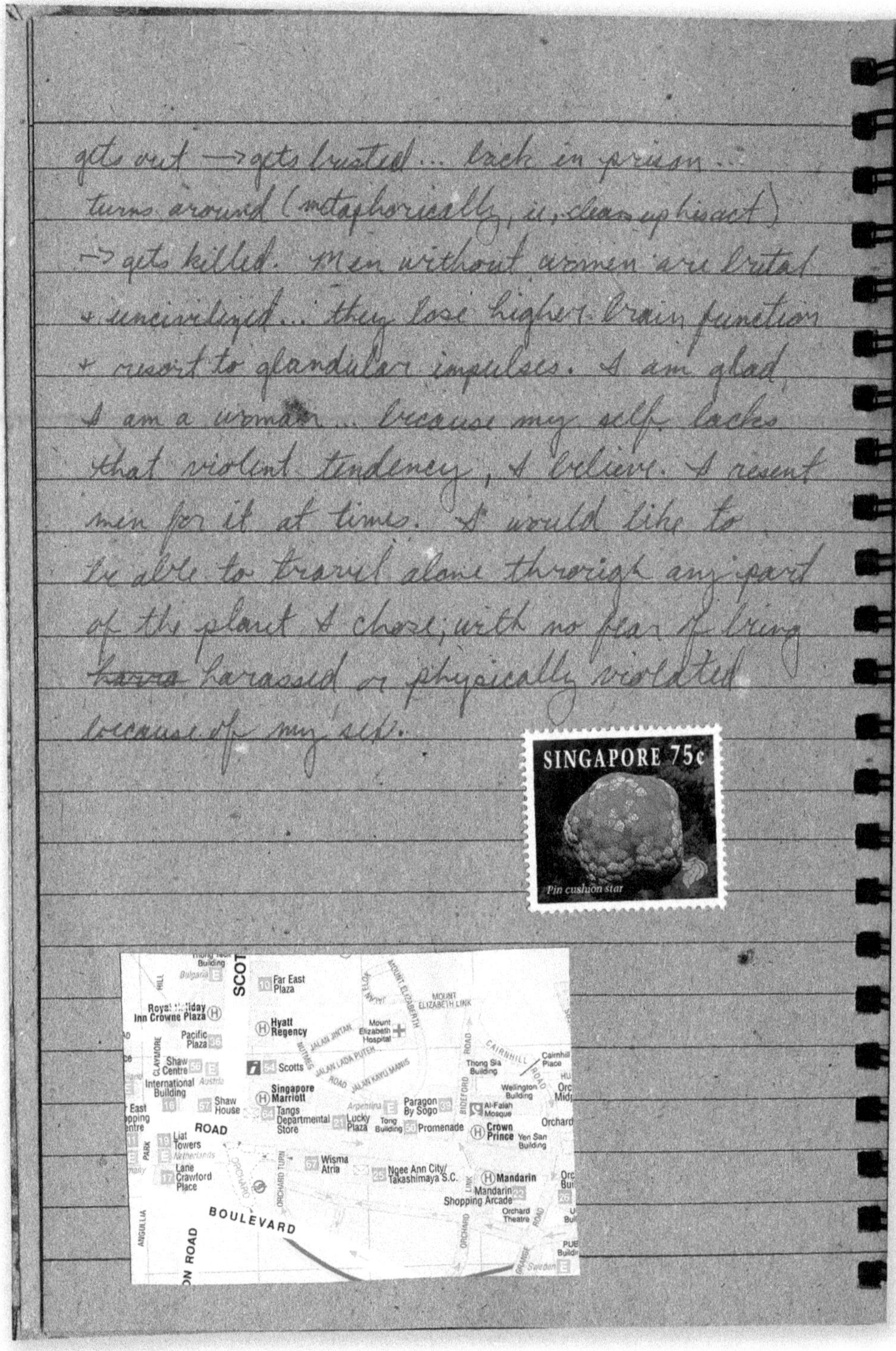

gets out → gets busted... back in prison...
turns around (metaphorically, i.e., cleans up his act)
→ gets killed. Men without women are brutal
+ uncivilized... they lose higher brain function
+ resort to glandular impulses. I am glad
I am a woman... because my self lacks
that violent tendency, I believe. I resent
men for it at times. I would like to
be able to travel alone through any part
of the planet I chose; with no fear of being
~~have~~ harassed or physically violated
because of my sex.

Hawker Centres
Durian: Love it or hate it, this spiky oval fruit is a favourite with Singaporeans. Some people find the smell of durians overpowering, and indeed they have been banned from public places in Singapore such as the Mass Rapid Transit. However, devotees just love the richness of this king of tropical fruits.
SINGAPORE
新加坡

our carriage was open, tucked our luggage away, + helped us to our seats. I gave him 100 rupees + he graciously smiled at me, folded his hands in front of him, tilted his head + ~~th~~ said "thank you very much." It was the equivalent of $3.^{00} .. he had carried more than what he weighed through the crowded depot, leading Vicki + A to our train .. we didn't have to ask anyone any questions, nor strain ourselves in anyway... There was something unsettling about allowing this person to assume all the burden, but there was no stopping him .. which was his intent, .. and so we paid him well... what he had hoped for.

stuffed caspian, a paneer roll, + two orange sodas. It was very tasty + we were content.

People stare at us... not in an admiring way... they leer, to some extent. Today Vicki was wearing an outfit that looked like this . She was wearing tights + was well covered, I thought. But men stared at her legs the entire day. At one point in a rickshaw, the driver angled his rearview mirror down to view Vicki's crotch... like he could really see anything! The men do things like this, as if what Vicki was wearing was out of line, and yet they'll stop in the middle of the street + whip out their dicks + urinate... as if that's acceptable.

I was also sad because I would never see Assu again, nor would I ever have the relationship with him again that I had that first hour in Varanasi before money ever exchanged between us.

I sat outside of our hotel, on the wall overlooking the field. I saw his little brother, easily reckognizable by the golden green eyes. And then I saw Assu. He sat next to me on the wall. Two other rickshaw drivers came over... "You have the same eyes" one of them said. "No, mine are blue, his are green." I said.

I asked Assu if he knew where we could get money exchanged.

"Yes."

"Can we walk there?"

"Yes."

He walked with us to get our U.S. dollars changed into Rupees & showed

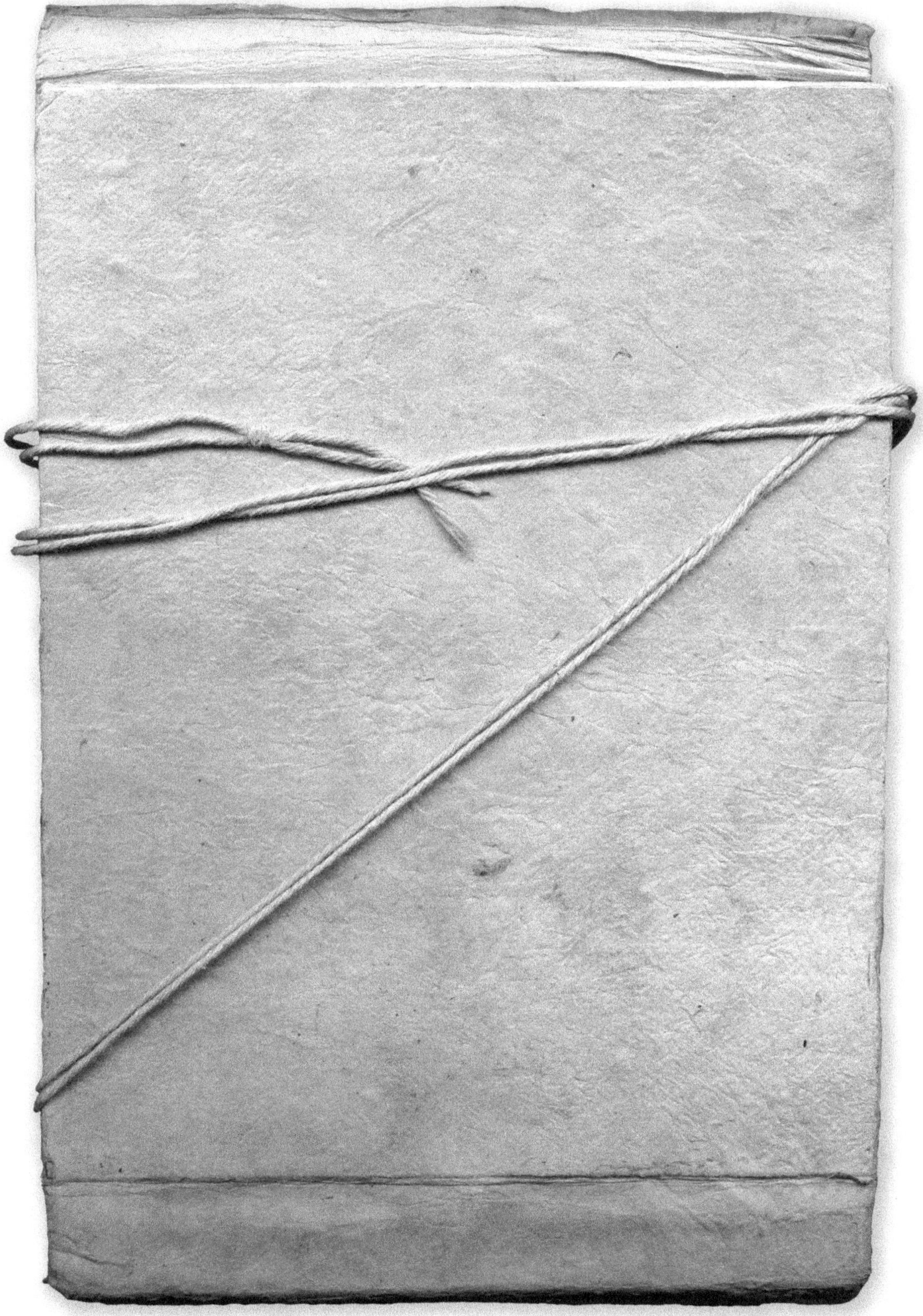

12/31/94 The last day of 1994 ... and I'm thrilled to see it come to a close. We are in Pushkar sitting by the lake. We arrived last evening after a very tenuous journey which set tempers and emotions in a flurry between Vicki, Barry, + myself. The past few days have been somewhat tense, as I felt that Vicki was slipping into a foul mood... deeper and deeper. Finally, yesterday afternoon in the car when we arrived in Jaipur, Vicki seemed to snap a bit at something I said + I caught her on it.. I just needed to know what was going on in her mind. At the same instance, Barry turned around and said, "Vicki, for the past two days you have been the moodiest fucking person I have ever met in my life!" At that point my heart plummeted to my gut.. Vicki was totally caught off guard, and tears welled up in her eyes, + she said "Obviously you two have already had a conversation about this." We hadn't. The timing was awful + I felt absolutely awful because it looked as if the only two people Vicki had to turn to for any kind of emotional consolation had venomously turned against her. All I wanted to do was pacify her + I immediately shifted my intent and went to grab her hand, but she withdrew it and said, "That was cold, that was so cold," + looked absolutely crushed + confused. She got out of the car, Barry got out of the car, I was panicked + finally got out of the car. Barry said, "I'm going to go off for about an hour + I'll meet you two back here," meaning the restaurant that the driver had stopped in front of. I went over to Vicki + she said, "I'm outa here... I'm leaving," and she was ready and determined to have the driver take her to the train station to catch the next one to Delhi. I convinced her to come inside the restaurant for the next 30 minutes to calm down before she left and when she sat down at the table she burst into sobs... my heart broke for her, because I realized what I had mistaken as a sour mood was actually pent up depression and anxiety. I felt like I had done her a grave injustice, and abandoned her when she needed me most. For the next hour Vicki unloaded her grief and I tried to console her. I apologized over + over again for myself misreading her, and for Barry's unnecessary + harsh comment. I told her I had no idea how sad she was + that she should have let me know. She was homesick... tired of dealing with people hassling + hounding her in the streets of India... affected by the state of the people + the animals. She was ready to leave. I agreed she should, but not on the next train. She decided to go to Pushkar + leave thereafter as soon as possible.

I felt that Barry's comment to Vicki was very unnecessary and I was angry. It's one thing for me to say something to her, having known her for ten years, but to have a person that has only spent a number of days with you lash out like that... I wouldn't have taken it well. Vicki told me that it hurt, his comment, because she really liked and respected him, + didn't have any inkling that he felt so strongly about her attitude.

1/12/95 Bangkok

I wrote in a postcard to my brother that Bangkok is "fairly [illegible] ... has incredible food and interesting clubs where women do some very [illegible] things with their Kegle muscles. Last night, I asked Barry if we could see one of the "pussy shows." [illegible] was in the frame of mind to exercise my scientific observational tendencies. The night before, we had visited Pat Pong, where all of the "working girl" clubs are located. Barry took me into a club (at my request) where some Thai girls were dancing on an elevated platform in the center of the bar. There were about seven girls dancing, unenthusiastically ... all in bathing suits ... about 3 one pieces + the rest in fairly scant bikinis. One of the women was very beautiful and smiled when I smiled at her. One of the girls looked prepubescent and couldn't have been more than 13 or 14 ... all looked under the age of 20. Although these girls were dancing unenthusiastically, they would interact amongst themselves, laughing with one another and acting like "girls." They were all very pretty. In the bar, there were about a dozen girls, all wearing bathing suits, sitting with, mingling with, the western men. The environment, at worst, was tacky ... but it wasn't sleazy. The "working girls" were just that ... working girls. This was their job and they seemed to be making the best of it.

The "pussy bar" wasn't that much different, in terms of attitude of the girls ... again, they seemed to be having a good time amongst themselves, but generally performed without enthusiasm ... it was a "clinical" performance which included the following:

1) Women dancing in thong bikini's topless.

2) Woman that opened a bottle with her vagina (she aided this process with her fingers, covertly)

4) A man and a woman having sex: this deserves a brief description ... The bar lights were dimmed red ... a man and woman got up on the platform in their underwear ... soft music was playing (the theme song from "Ghost"). They took off each others underware + layed side by side on the floor of the platform. The girl began massaging the boys penis with her [illegible] then gave him a blow job (I think this was to get him erect). The facial expressions [illegible] performers were of utter apathy. The ~~[illegible]~~ man then laid on his back, the girl [illegible] him + placed his penis inside her vagina. Within a 3 minute period, they covered [illegible] position in the Kama Sutra, maintaining coitus the entire time, facial expressions [never] changing. Then they stopped, hopped off the platform, + dressed, right next to [where] Barry + I were sitting.

5) Pussy bowling (Barry was glad they had a sporting event included in the program). [In] this event, each girl took what looked like a pair of chopstix, wrapped one end in [a wad] of toilette paper + inserted it up her vagina, so the sticks were hanging out.

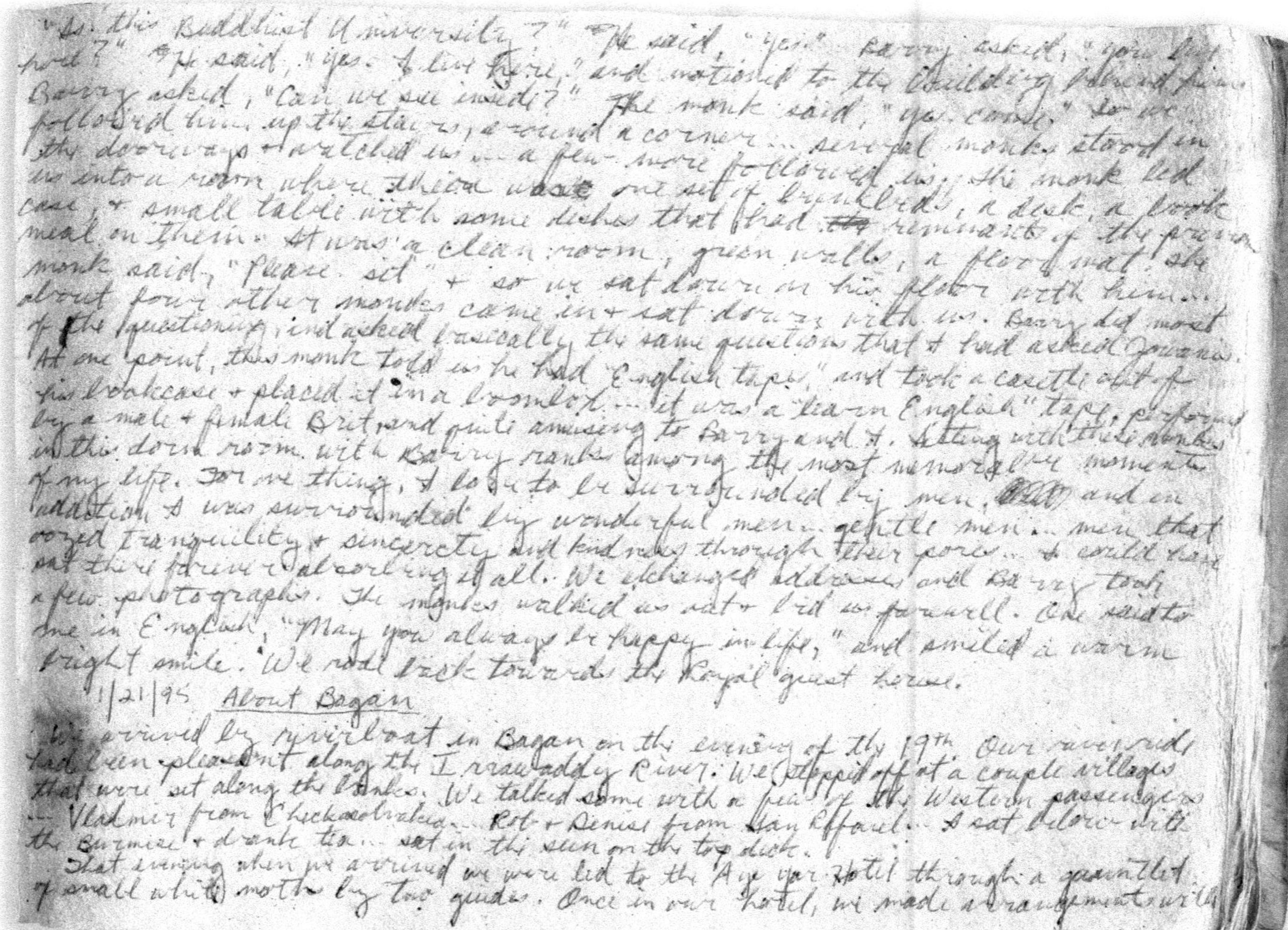

"Is this Buddhist University?" He said, "yes." Barry asked, "you live here?" He said, "yes. I live here," and motioned to the building behind him. Barry asked, "Can we see inside?" The monk said, "yes. come." So we followed him up the stairs, around a corner... several monks stood in the doorways + watched us... a few more followed us; the monk led us into a room where there was one set of bunk beds, a desk, a book case, + small table with some dishes that had remnants of the previous meal on them. It was a clean room, green walls, a floor mat. The monk said, "please sit" + so we sat down on the floor with him... about four other monks came in + sat down with us. Barry did most of the questioning, and asked basically the same questions that I had asked Gowana. At one point, this monk told us he had "English tapes," and took a cassette out of his bookcase + placed it in a boombox... it was a "learn English" tape, performed by a male + female Brit and quite amusing to Barry and I. Sitting with these monks in this dorm room with Barry ranks among the most memorable moments of my life. For one thing, I love to be surrounded by men, and in addition I was surrounded by wonderful men... gentle men... men that oozed tranquility + sincerity and kindness through their pores... I could have sat there forever absorbing it all. We exchanged addresses and Barry took a few photographs. The monks walked us out + bid us farewell. One said to me in English, "May you always be happy in life," and smiled a warm bright smile. We rode back towards the Royal guest house.

1/21/95 About Bagan

We arrived by riverboat in Bagan on the evening of the 19th. Our river ride had been pleasant along the Irrawaddy River. We stopped off at a couple villages that were set along the banks. We talked some with a few of the Western passengers... Vladimir from Czechoslovakia... Rob + Denise from San Rafael... I sat below with the Burmese + drank tea... sat in the sun on the top deck.

That evening when we arrived we were led to the Aye Yar Hotel through a gauntlet of small white moths by two guides. Once in our hotel, we made arrangements with

2/1/95 Vientienne, Laos.

Before I get into Laos, a few words about Koh Samui, Thailand. Koh Samui is an island off of the south east coast of Thailand. We stayed at a place called the Fair Guest House. It was absolutely beautiful, this island, and the Fair Guest House bungalow we stayed in was perfect... right on the beach... Chaweng Beach... beautiful aquamarine water, white sand beach, coconut palms, sunshine + balmy air. A woman was giving massages on the beach... a man grilled corn on the cob w/ butter + salt for you + Another woman came by with cold drinks and snacks! We sat on the beach + read. At night, we ate scrumptious Thai food at the Oriental restaurant after drinking a beer first + playing backgammon at the bar next door. After dinner, we sat + had a drink at the "lady-man" bar, where some very masculine looking transsexuals flaunted their pseudo-feminism. We then went to the Green Mango Bar + drank + made out + went back to our bungalow + had sex. This was our routine for four days, three nights. We also rented motorbikes + cruised around the island. The last day, we sat in the morning (Monday, Jan 30) at the Bauhaus Bar + watched San Francisco 49ers absolutely kill the San Diego Chargers in the Superbowl. We flew out that afternoon for Bangkok. That evening in Bangkok we ate at the Lemon Grass Restaurant (DIVINE) + then went to one of the go-go bars across from the Nana Hotel. One of the dancers who we had talked with before we left for Koh Samui came up to me + placed her hand on my leg + began talking with us. She was a very pretty girl... cute little body, sweet face with a wide smile + high cheekbones. She told me my hair was pretty + began to brush it...

<u>Vientienne</u> - When we first returned to Bangkok (before leaving for Koh Samui) Barry told me he had a surprise + would tell me in a week what it was. So for the entire week he entertained himself by giving me misleading hints about what the surprise was, and he would constantly provoke my interest in the surprise by "bringing it up" or asking me to "guess." He is such an imp!

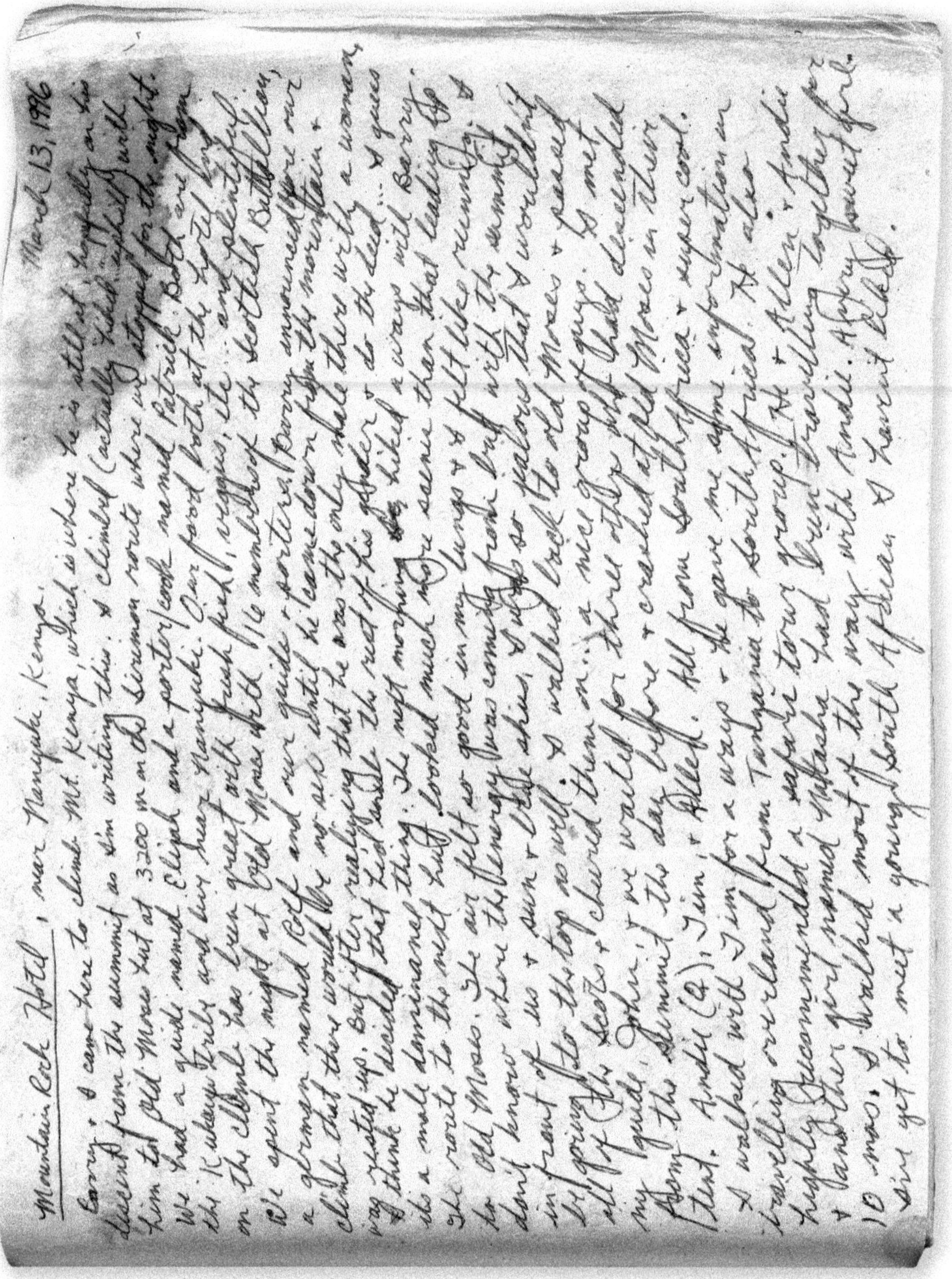
Mountain Rock Hotel, near Nanyuki, Kenya. March 13, 1996

Barry + I came here to climb Mt. Kenya, which is where he is still at, hopefully on his descent from the summit as I'm writing this. I climbed (actually "hiked" uphill) with him to Old Moses hut at 3200 m on the Sirimon route where we stopped for the night. We had a guide named Elijah and a porter/cook named Patrick. Both are from the Kikuyu tribe and live near Nanyuki. Our food both at the hotel and on the climb has been great with fresh fish, veggies, etc... and plentiful. We spent the night at Old Moses with 16 members of the Scottish Battallion, a German named Rolf and our guide + porters. Barry announced before our climb that there would be no sex until he came down from the mountain + was rested up. But after realizing that he was the only male there with a woman, I think he decided that he'd snub the rest of his gender + do the deed... I guess its a male dominance thing. The next morning I hiked a ways with Barry. The route to the next hut looked much more scenic than that leading up to Old Moses. The air felt so good in my lungs + I felt like running. I don't know where the energy was coming from but with the summit in front of us + sun + blue skies, I was so jealous that I wouldn't be going to the top as well. I walked back to Old Moses + passed all of the Scots + cheered them on... a nice group of guys. I met my guide, John, + we waited for three others who had descended from the summit the day before + crashed at Old Moses in their tent. Andie (♀), Jim, + Allen. All from South Africa + super cool. I walked with Jim for a ways + he gave me some information on travelling overland from Tanzania to South Africa. He also highly recommended a safari tour group. He + Allen + Andie + another girl named Natasha had been travelling together for 10 mos. I walked most of the way with Andie. A very sweet girl. I've yet to meet a young South African I haven't liked.

In the end, the owner agreed to refund half of our [illegible]

3/23/96 Mt. Kilimanjaro! Our arrival into Moshi was mu[illegible] Arusha's. Barry had wanted to contact M.E.M. for arra[illegible] we were walking to our hotel, we met a man from M.E.M[illegible] arrangements with them. The owner's name was Mohamad and [illegible] other Tanzanians. He had travelled extensively through Africa + [illegible] the continent... Europe (Germany), U.S., Canada. He grew up in Zanzibar + had tried his entrepreneurial skills in several different ways + places. But his tour agency in Moshi, is bound to be a success because he clearly uses foresight + has an understanding of efficiency + what the average Western tourist wants out of a safari or climb. He definitely is a businessman at heart... still, there's something about him that is questionable.

Mt. Kilimanjaro is what I expected in beauty + attraction. The hike through the forest was lush, and mountain wildflowers were still in bloom here + there. We saw several elusive Colobus monkeys jumping from tree to tree, with their white tails hanging down. I feel very sad that I won't be hiking to the top of the mountain as everyone here seems to have that as their goal, and so I feel quite alienated. The mountain is very magnetic and while I know the summit is probably out of my league, I would have loved to have hiked up further to the next set of huts at least. I understand why people climb mountains... there's something very pulling in them and the feeling of the changes that occur in your body as you ascend is wonderful. The hikes I did on Mt. Kenya + Mt. Kilimanjaro were some of the best because my body felt so good. It was invigorating and I so badly wanted to maintain that feeling of euphoria, but in the end always had to descend,... sadly. Sitting around + talking with the other people who were climbing the mountain (Kili) was great + there were several very interesting women that I would have enjoyed spending more time with. But the main thing was continuing on. I just wanted to keep climbing + hiking up, with the weather unusually dry + warm, the conditions on the mountain were ideal.

6:35 pm. Kilimanjaro is framed by my window. The clouds have receded + the summit is clear, with the evening sun casting a sweet girl. When the police were arguing with the Prince [illegible] with a pad of paper + pencil + asked me for my address in [illegible] write to me... go figure.

On Tanzania 30/3/96

In Zanzibar, the architecture is an influence of Arab + Indian styles. You can walk through narrow streets + see elaborate doors, hand carved + studded, and balconies above you with pointed windows in the back. Most of the buildings are in a state of decay, but they still are beautiful + give the island a sense of cultural asthetic. Zanzibar is almost entirely Moslem and many of the women wear veils + "body sacks." Almost every tourist spending time in Tanzania ends up in Zanzibar, usually at the end of their journey and it seems logical as you want to leave a country on an "up note", and the island offers that + redeems Tanzania to a small extent. I have found very little about Tanzania + its people that I can praise, regretfully. It's easier to convey generalizations about a country when they're positive, but one writes negative generalizations reluctantly about a country + culture, especially when the people are of a different color because it becomes interpreted as racist, which in part, is true. But through my travels in Tanzania, I have continually searched for the positive aspects of the culture + I have found almost nothing. There have been a few Tanzanians that we've met who have impressed us as individuals, but in general, I've found the majority to be lacking... in motivation, intellect, pride, and warmth. They are sexist and racist + feel no sense of guilt in failing to honor their word or commitments. I don't believe that these characteristics are a result of the race, but rather of the culture. The potential for improvement definitately lies in each individual, with his maize seeds if he didn't use his fertalizer he told her he had eaten them... that he had washed the pestacide off + used the maize to feed his family...

Mayra + Vic took Barry + I for a boat ride on the Zambezi river at sunset. We sat afterwards with them + Grams + Mayoras daughters at their boat club + had a beer.

Barry + I also went white water river rafting on the Zambezi River + had a splash! I met a girl on the raft with us that had been attacked at Nakhata Bay. The guy tried to rob her + then hit her on the base of her skull/neck with a mashetti... she almost died... horrific story.

Almost every house we passed in Vic Falls had one or two dogs in their yard ☺.

17-4-96 Windhoek, Namibia: Barry + I hitched rides all the way from the border of Zimbabwe to here - Windhoek, Nabibia. From Vic Falls, we took a taxi to the border... then from the Zimbabwe border to the Botswana border, we hopped in the cab of a huge cargo truck. Then we went a short way in the back of a pickup truck to the junction towards Ngoma Bridge. After waiting for about an hour, we took a lost cab ride to the main road towards Ngoma Bridge where we caught a ride on the back of a pickup truck with about 4 Black men. At Ngoma, we caught a ride again on the back of a pickup with a western couple + their 4 month old baby. We ended up riding with Annie + Joshua from Katima Mullio all the way to Popa Falls, stopping

Menu from Wagamama, 2009

desserts

14	**mango with lime zest and lychee sorbet** v	£3.10
15	* **tamarind and chilli pavlova** v served with a raspberry and tamarind sauce	£4.60
16	* **coconut reika** v three scoops of coconut ice cream topped with mango sauce and coconut flakes	£3.20
17	* **white chocolate and ginger cheesecake** v served with a chilli toffee ginger sauce	£4.50
18	* **chocolate fudge cake** v served with dark chocolate wasabi sauce and vanilla pod ice cream	£4.50
19	**natural fruit ice lollies** v ask your server for today's choice	£1.50

tea

		£1.30
712	breakfast blend	
713	earl grey	
714	blackcurrant, ginseng and vanilla	
714	peppermint	

coffee

730	americano	£1.65
731	cappuccino	£1.95
732	latte	£1.95
733	espresso	£1.35
734	double espresso	£1.55
735	extra shot	.20
736	iced coffee	£1.95
	decaf available	
745	**hot chocolate**	£1.95

all drinks are available to take-out

* these desserts contain dairy products and may contain traces of nuts

v these dishes are suitable for vegetarians

Letter to Jackie from Barry on Back of Menu, 2009

10-8-09 6:30 AM, LADBROKE ARMS, LONDON, ENGLAND

DEAR JACKIE:

I FIGURE A LETTER HAS A BETTER CHANCE OF GETTING READ, NO?

I AM SITTING IN THE LADBROKE ARMS, DRINKING A PINT, WAITING THE MENU TO ORDER DINNER.

I AM THINKING OF YOU A LOT TODAY, ALL NICE THOUGHTS I ASSURE YOU... SO MUCH THAT IT KIND OF HURTS A BIT. EST-CE QUE CAS C'EST L'AMOUR JE ME DEMANDE? OUI, JE LE CROIS!

WHAT A WHIRLWIND! ARRIVING IN LONDON, JET-LAGGED, TO A NOTE FOR ME TO CALL YOU. I GO TO SLEEP UNSURE WHETHER OR NOT I WILL SEE YOU IN LONDON THE NEXT DAY. YOU ARRIVE, WE DO A "SURPRISE TOUR" WAGAMAMA, LADBROKE ARMS, ORSELLES, ALL PLACES WHERE I HAVE GREAT MEMORIES OF US! THAT NIGHT ON PEUT DE L'AMOUR. THE NEXT DAY YOU HAVE COFFEE W/CYNTHIA. WE MEET IN HAMPSTEAD AND GO THROUGH THE HEATH TO HIGHGATE... TADPOLE COTTAGE, ANOTHER PLACE WITH GREAT MEMORIES OF LITTLE BENJAMIN GROWING UP! CHECK OUT A MUSEUM, A WALK THROUGH HYDE PARK AND BACK FOR A GREAT DINNER WITH CYNTHIA AND ALLAN. SO GREAT TO HANG OUT WITH FRIENDS WITH AN "OUTSIDE-[illegible]" PERSPECTIVE. SATURDAY COFFEE IN HAMPSTEAD AND THEN OFF TO CHELSEA FOR LUNCH WITH CAIN. A QUICK VISIT WITH CLARE AND THEN WE TAKE YOU TO SOME SPECTRAL HEALING WITH ANN JONES. A WALK TO KNIGHTSBRIDGE, DINNER AT A GREAT LEBANESE RESTAURANT, BACK TO THE HOTEL TO CHANGE & BACK TO KNIGHTSBRIDGE TO THE BLUE BAR. GREAT ATMOSPHERE, GREAT COMPANY, GREAT CONVERSATION! ET PUIS APRÈS ENCORE L'AMOUR. SUNDAY, ANOTHER MORNING FOR COFFEE IN HAMPSTEAD AND THEN OFF TO THE EUROSTAR. TRAIN TO PARIS & ILE ST. LOUIS AGAIN, WHAT A GREAT PLACE! FUNNY GUY AT THE HOTEL AND A RUDE WAITER AT THE BRASSERIE, SO TYPICAL. WALKING EVERYWHERE IN PARIS, WHAT GREAT SIGHTS! WHAT GREAT DINNERS. CAN'T REMEMBER THE LAST TIME WE ATE SO WELL. MORNING COFFEES AT THE EDGE OF THE ISLAND. REMEMBER LITTLE ELLA SITTING ON YOUR LAP? TRAIN BACK FROM PARIS. SO NICE TO HAVE A SPECIAL DINNER WITH YOU AT THE LADBROKE ARMS! WHAT A GREAT TRIP, GREAT COMPANY, HOW REFRESHING. I AM STILL SOAKING IN IT!

JACKIE, WE HAVE BEEN THROUGH SO MUCH OF OUR LIVES TOGETHER. I HAVE KNOWN YOU NOW ALMOST 30 YEARS (29 TO BE EXACT). IT HAS BEEN MORE THAN 20 YEARS SINCE I TRIED TO STEAL A KISS ON YOU AND YOUR INTERESTING TRIP TO NY W/ YOUR BOYFRIEND. IT HAS BEEN ALMOST 15 YEARS SINCE THOSE MAGICAL TIMES IN LONDON WITH YOU. WE HAVE BEEN MARRIED NOW FOR MORE THAN 12 YEARS. WE HAVE HAD SOME GREAT EXPERIENCES AND MEMORIES. WE HAVE MORE RECENTLY HAD SOME CHALLENGES. I THINK IT IS A TESTAMENT TO US THAT WE HAVE MADE THE EFFORT TO WORK THROUGH THEM. AS A RESULT, I BELIEVE WE ARE AT THE POINT OF MOVING OUR MARRIAGE TO A NEW AND EVEN BETTER LEVEL. I KNOW THAT THERE MAY BE SETBACKS ALONG THE WAY, BUT I BELIEVE THAT WE HAVE SO MUCH TO LOOK FORWARD TO TOGETHER BOTH AS A FAMILY AND AS A MARRIED [illegible]

WITH LOVE,

XO, HUBBY

"Plato advised teachers to take advantage of this natural longing for beauty. Present more and more beautiful objects to students, and so form their imaginations in such a way that as they age they will desire more and more serious things. Start by presenting a student with a beautiful face. Once he has appreciated physical beauty, he will be grasped by higher beauty, which is the beauty of lovely personality and a good person's lovely heart. And when he has understood that, he will grasp even higher beauty, which is the beauty of a just society... And when he has seen that, he will hunger for a higher beauty still, which is the search for truth and wisdom, and when he has seen that, he will feel a longing for the ultimate form of beauty, which is beauty itself, the everlasting form of all-encompassing transcendent beauty, which neither flowers nor fades, to which nothing can be added and from which nothing can be subtracted—which for Plato was divinity itself."

From DailyStoic.com

CPSIA information can be obtained
at www.ICGtesting.com
Printed in the USA
BVHW022119241019
562003BV00001B/2/P

9 780996 559065